I0794211

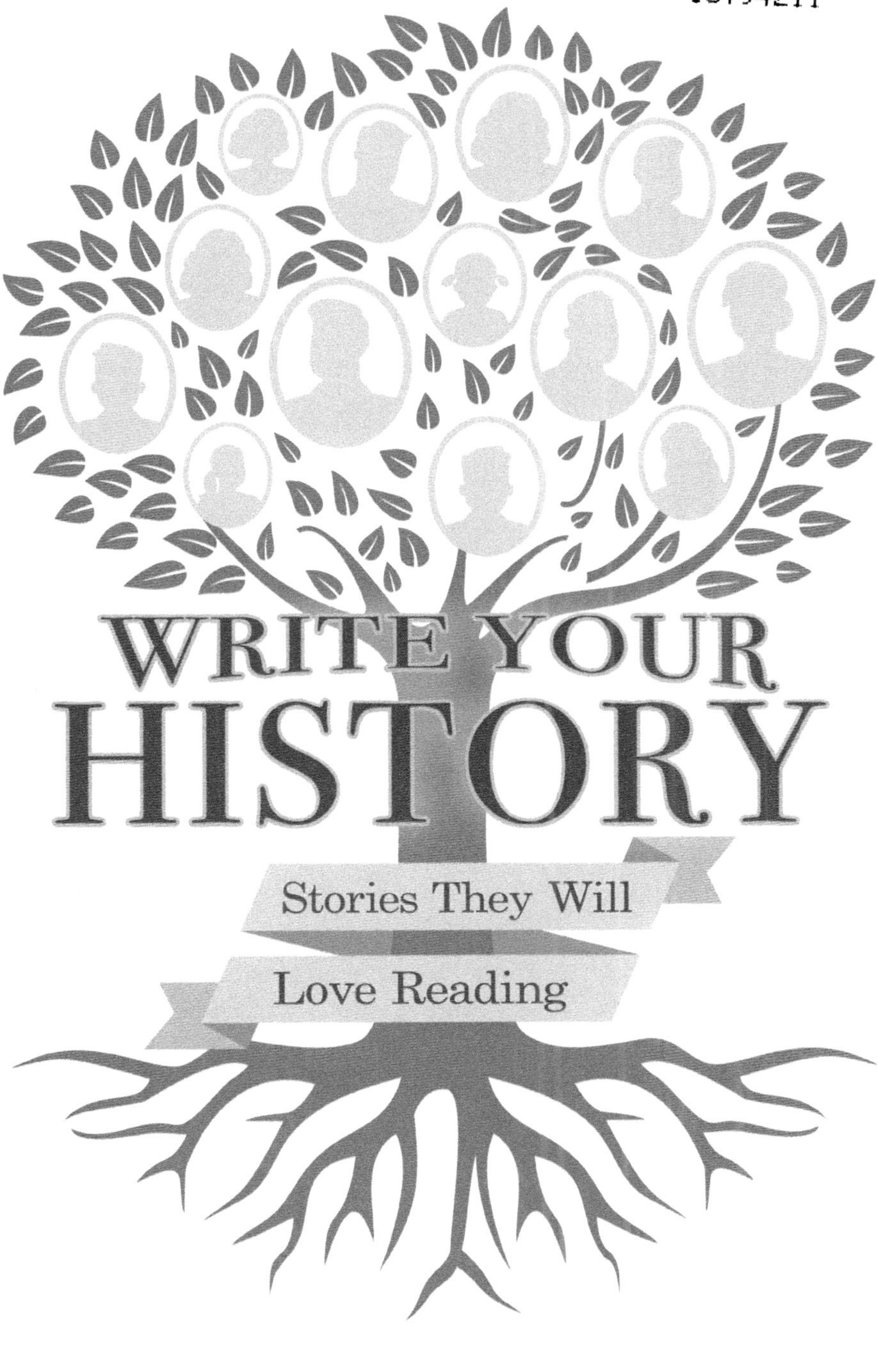

WRITE YOUR HISTORY

Stories They Will Love Reading

What others are saying about this book

I have long felt the desire to write about my history and family, yet I lacked the basic skills and confidence to do so. However, as I have listened to the thoughts and concepts that Janet introduces in this book, I have been able to write more of my history than I thought possible. As you read *Write Your History*, you will receive thoughts on what and how, and as you act on those thoughts, you will not only become a better writer but also find joy in the process.

—LEON JENSEN, former student of the author

Write Your History is definitely something to read and ponder. I had the chance to study Janet's book and utilize the suggestions and other things it shares. It helped me look at things from a different perspective and to know that there is more than one way to write my story. Sometimes writing a history can seem like a big task and something that requires a lot of effort. *Write Your History* gives suggestions, examples, and quotes that helped me understand that a history doesn't have to be long and perfect but just a moment in my life. It made me realize how important it is to write something, no matter how small or long, not only for myself, but also for those who follow. Even if I didn't have children, others might read some of my accounts and learn something. The quotes, stories, and examples in this book make it unique like nothing I've read before. I highly recommend it to anyone. Regardless of whether you are a writer or not, there is something in this book for everyone.

—DENIS FRANCESCO MODUGNO, family history specialist and a consultant for one of the major family history companies in the world

Janet E. Winward

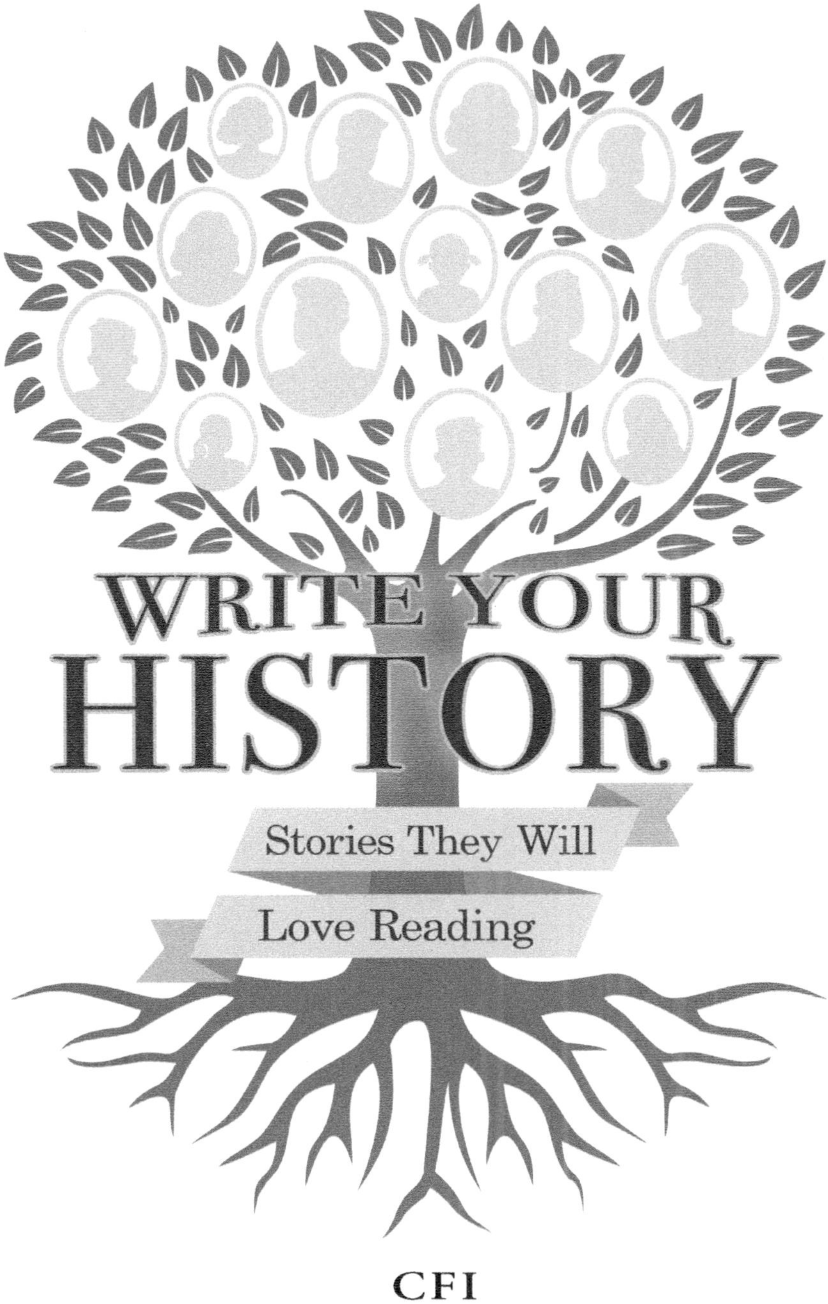

WRITE YOUR HISTORY

Stories They Will Love Reading

CFI
An imprint of Cedar Fort, Inc.
Springville, Utah

© 2023 Janet E. Winward
All rights reserved.

No part of this book may be reproduced in any form whatsoever, whether by graphic, visual, electronic, film, microfilm, tape recording, or any other means, without prior written permission of the publisher, except in the case of brief passages embodied in critical reviews and articles.

This is not an official publication of The Church of Jesus Christ of Latter-day Saints. The opinions and views expressed herein belong solely to the author and do not necessarily represent the opinions or views of Cedar Fort, Inc. Permission for the use of sources, graphics, and photos is also solely the responsibility of the author.

ISBN 13: 978-1-4621-4487-7

Published by CFI, an imprint of Cedar Fort, Inc.
2373 W. 700 S., Suite 100, Springville, UT 84663
Distributed by Cedar Fort, Inc., www.cedarfort.com

Library of Congress Control Number: 2022950678

Cover design by Shawnda T. Craig
Cover design © 2023 Cedar Fort, Inc.
Edited and typeset by Liz Kazandzhy

Printed in the United States of America

10 9 8 7 6 5 4 3 2 1

Printed on acid-free paper

Dedication

This book really is the work of a lot higher power than me. I totally credit heaven for anything that can or will help you. It is written to help God's children fulfill our responsibility to record our lives. Thus, it is dedicated to building the kingdom of God on earth, one baby step at a time. This is my current little drop in the bucket of earthly efforts.

This book is also dedicated to everyone who has any desire to write and build their life stories; to so many who have encouraged me with words of strength and gratitude; to anyone who cares about the next generations; and to those who will hopefully be the beneficiaries of all our efforts.

This book is dedicated to my wonderful husband who always believed in me and encouraged me. I have felt his love, strength, and encouragement. Sometimes when I would get discouraged, I could hear him from his home in heaven saying, "You can do it."

And you can too.

CONTENTS

Acknowledgments

I want to recognize all my students who have encouraged me by taking what I have given them and building their life stories, and who have also encouraged me to write this book so others can learn what they have been able to learn. It has been a great adventure and a marvelous privilege to work with so many talented people who just need a few bits of knowledge and encouragement themselves. Watching them grow has lifted and strengthened me, giving me courage.

A few of my students have consented to let you read their stories. You will find them in Part III of this book. I am amazed that they have used what I've shared to accomplish what I would call success in this endeavor.

May the Lord bless many others as you use this book to help your life stories come into existence. I have faith in you. You can do this. The Lord will help you.

Introduction

Your life is full of stories. Your goal should be to write a history full of strength-building experiences. My goal is to help you to write those stories so they will lift and strengthen your descendants. Together we should be able to create for your posterity a wealth of strength-building stories to help them maneuver the rough spots and trials of their lives, and to believe they have the strengths needed to withstand the storms of their life. In order to do that, you will learn how to write in ways that may seem different but really aren't. Your life is full a great examples to lift you and others, but it won't help them if they don't read it. Recognize and accept the stories that fill your life.

I sincerely believe that your life can and will influence others, both now and later. The Lord cannot put your stories into the hands of those who will benefit from them if *you* don't write them.

It is not my intention to teach you to be a professional writer. My hope is that you will learn how to be yourself and put it on paper—that you will learn how to pull the stories out of your life and share them with your families in a way that they will enjoy reading them. My goal is for you to write in a way that your readers will be able to learn from your accomplishments and weaknesses enough that they can be a little better able to handle their trials with more personal strength, because you shared your learned strengths with them through your stories. Their lives are going to be difficult enough without repeating your mistakes—they will be easier if they learn how you survived hard times. You can strengthen those who mean the most to you and those who *will* mean the most to you in the future.

May the Lord bless many as you use this information to help your life stories come into existence on paper, recording strengths that are needed both now and always.

I wish you all a wonderful life, and I hope for you the determination to record that wonderful life for posterity, through stories from your own life and those of your ancestors.

I wish you love and strength in your endeavors. I believe in you.

To you may I say, "You can do this!" I have faith in you. The Lord will help you.

PART I

WRITING YOUR HISTORY

Why?

Why should I bother to write my personal history? It's a lot of work. Besides, I can't remember anything worth writing.

In part, it's because of this: "In every conceivable manner, the family is link to our past, bridge to our future."[1]

If the family is the link, what is your responsibility as an important part of that link? May I suggest that it's to build that bridge. How are you going to do that? By sharing stories—stories of the lives of your readers' ancestors, and that includes *you*!

How? This book is written for that reason—to help you know how. This book will make it easier for you to write, give you memory triggers to help bring out your life stories, and help you make your stories interesting to those you hope will read it so that they will keep reading once they start.

And most importantly, *why* do you need to write? What's in it for you, and who else will benefit? You will see for yourself.

Our prophet, President Russell M. Nelson, said, "It's wonderful to turn the hearts of the children to their fathers by telling important family history stories in ways that are accessible and memorable."[2]

Children are drawn to meaningful family stories and learning about family culture, family recipes, and experiences from their ancestors. Actually, they also love to learn about their own parents and others they know. These stories give them strength for their own lives. They won't even realize what you're giving them—they will just enjoy the stories.

You have a responsibility to those who come after you, your descendants. If you are single, you have or will have other family. You care about them. You want to be with them even after this life. What can you do to help them be the very best people they can be? You can write your personal history.

How is that going to help? You can give them strength that is more personal. Just like we gain strength from the scriptures and other stories, they can also gain strength from their ancestor—you!

Writing will also give you strength for your trials. It can help you to accept that you're better than you think you are.

May I also suggest you listen to or read the talk by Elder Dale G. Renlund called "Consider the Goodness and Greatness of God."[3] Elder Renlund discusses several blessings that come as we reflect on God's influence in our lives, which we surely do when we write our personal histories.

In time, you will find other reasons to record your history, but let's start with just these two. First, the Lord has commanded us to keep a record (see D&C 21:1; 3 Nephi 27:23). And second, we will be judged "out of the books which shall be written" (2 Nephi 19:11).

I'm going to stick in another reason here: to improve your children's (and ancestors') sense of belonging. In Part III of this book, you will find a short synopsis of one research study in the section "Research Study: 'The Stories That Bind Us'" (page 140). The whole study is available from *The New York Times*, but the gist of it is that the more children know about their family history, the more emotionally resilient they are. What a blessing that can come from you recording your history!

I know you might face many road blocks on your journey, but I promise you it's worth the effort and the necessary adaptations and creativity. Plus, it can be fun. Do it for them *and* for you.

In the last part of this book, you will find some stories that may help you under the *why* and *how* of writing your personal history.

Happy writing! Look for the fun. Think about your descendants, but enjoy it for you.

"Each one of us is the custodian of one first-class story, the story of [our] own life. Every human life is a story [and] is interesting if it can be conveyed."

—Stephen Leacock[4]

I totally believe this, and that is why I want to teach you how to make your life story conveyable and interesting.

"One day, the story you write of how you overcame what you went through will be someone's survival guide as they face their own storms."

—Janet

How?

If you really think about your life, you will find it is full of stories. It *is* stories.

The first thing to remember is this: do *not* try to write in chronological order. You may wish to put your stories in that order later, but your memory doesn't work in that order, so don't try to write that way.

As you go through this book, you will think of stories in your life. The time for you write that story is when it comes to mind. It may or may not be one that fits the subject you are reading about, but that doesn't matter. Write it when it comes—don't wait!

"But what if I don't have time at that moment," you might ask. That's okay, but at least take a minute to write yourself a very careful note so that you will remember later what it was about and what you remembered.

"Okay," you say, "but I don't know *how* to write a story." Just keep reading.

Can you tell a story? Have you ever told a story to a child? Have you ever told anyone anything about your life? Well, you just told a story! Now write it.

I will teach you how to use lists to improve your memory and help you build your stories into something they will enjoy reading. You can't learn it all in one truck load any more than I can teach you that way. Be patient with yourself.

As you go through this book, you will learn step by step. You will be surprised in a year how good you really are at writing your stories. Hang in there.

Whatever you do, do *not* give up on yourself. The Lord won't and neither will I. Together we can do this. The Lord wants us to record our lives, and He never asks anything that isn't possible. We can do this. He has faith in us.

I'll give you a few things to remember that will help make your stories interesting, but I won't do it all at once. Here are some right now, but *don't* feel overwhelmed by all this. We will work on these things one at a time. Don't try to do it all now.

Here are some tips for now:

- Use a lot of descriptions. (For help, refer to the "Adjectives" list on page 138.)
- Colors can add a lot of "color" to your story.

- Sometimes shapes can help.
- Explain how something worked so they will be able to visualize.
- Use details.
- A photo or drawing can be helpful.
- Include a little humor when it fits.
- Maybe even include a touch of romance in some places.
- Be sure you include how you felt—your feelings about what happened.
- What did you do about it?
- Did it change something?
- Can you see the setting? Will the reader be able to join you in the place because of your vivid description?
- Sometimes while describing, include the size of things to help emphasize.
- Your stories represent you. Make sure the readers are seeing the right person.
- Put your reader in your book by using the right words to draw them into the story.
- Remember to believe in yourself. You are a valuable person. Don't hide it.

"The difference between
the almost right word
and the right word is
really a large matter—
it's the difference between
the lightning bug and
the lightning."

—Mark Twain[5]

People

Ready? Okay, now let's get to work.

Remember, you are writing for posterity as well as for yourself. You're writing stories because that's what your life is, a series of stories, *and* because they will enjoy reading stories more than just data.

As a reminder, you're going to write whatever you remember *when* you remember it. You can organize it as you wish later. Don't try to work in chronological order. Remember that memory doesn't work that way.

Let's go with something everyone has in their life: people. Start building a list.

Start your list. List every family member you can think of: parents, siblings, aunts, uncles, and grandparents, as well as your spouse, children, grandchildren, in-laws, and so on. List everyone you know or knew, and add ones you didn't know—perhaps those who died before you were born but had an influence on your life. Keep going until you have exhausted your memory. As you build your list, go down the page so you can go back to add thoughts and details as they come to your mind. Double-spacing would be good also. Leave room to add later as your memories continue to spark. Put them in any order you feel inclined to.

Your page may begin to look something like this:

- Father - [name] - was always on the run
- Mother - [name] - perfect pitch singing voice
- Grandpa J - lived well into his nineties and never stopped
- Grandma B - also lived past ninety
- Siblings - five of them (add names now or later)
- Uncles and aunts

I was privileged to know a lot of family members, even great aunts and uncles. They were wonderful people. If you were so blessed, be sure to include at least names and maybe something about them. How were you related? How did you feel about them?

Allow yourself time to write family names and information. If you can't do it all at one time, that's fine. Come back and work some more later. This should not become a drudgery. Make it fun and squeeze in moments to write. Continue down the page until you can't think of another relative.

Start with others in your life, maybe on separate page: neighbors, friends, teachers, anyone who touched your life. List everyone you know or knew. Keep going until your memory is exhausted, but leave room at the bottom to add later if you decide to. As you're writing (or later), add little notes about things that pop into your thoughts as you write a name or who they were.

As you're writing this list, stories will begin to come to mind. Don't wait or ignore the thought; interrupt your list-making and write at least a paragraph reminder of the story that came. If you need to stop making the list to write the story, do it.

This will be a long list. You won't want to write about all of them, but it will get you thinking. For some, you may want to add places that fit with them. For example, Grandma and Grandpa's house would be an important part of your memories with them.

Allow memories to start to flow. Make notes near names if they're short, or use another page so have plenty of room. Continue remembering and writing until a story begins to form. A particular incident may start to blossom in your mind. Begin to take hold of that story. Let it grow in your memory. Remember it like you were there. Put yourself back in time.

Write all your thoughts. Don't judge what you might want to keep. Just write it down as it comes—everything.

As you begin to think of a story, start another list specifically for that story: a list of all the things that need to be included in the story. Include everything needed, like where it happened, when it was (maybe the year), who was involved, what led up to the story, and how it happened. If the story comes to you in such a way that you can just write the story without having to think about it anymore, go ahead and do it. There are no rules for writing. It's your life.

Don't expect yourself to complete this list in one week. It may take time. Add to it over the weeks or even years as you think about it. Don't be too hard on yourself. The Lord only expects you to do your best. You have no right to expect more of yourself than He expects of you. I sure don't.

When you were a child, did you have a special friend? When you wrote that name down, did lots of stories come to mind? Write one of those stories, and remember all the things to include to make it fun and interesting.

Maybe you've got more to write about friends. Go ahead and write all you want.

How about family? Do you have stories about trips to Grandma's house, or maybe a special uncle? Write about them. You may have lots of stories running around right now and you can't write them all fast enough. Remember, write a paragraph to remind you later.

Some stories you can easily just write. If you have one of those, write it. Most stories take a little more effort. If so, do the list thing again. Make a list of everything you can think about as you consider the story. You've heard these: who, what, when, where, why, and how.

Now take a list from one of the stories you just outlined and create a story. Details are important; be specific enough to bring your reader into the story. Make them part of it. You want them to feel like they were watching the scene from another world before they came to earth.

Most of us have lots of stories about grandparents. Don't be afraid to include as many as you want. As you share, your descendants will learn to love their ancestors, and they will learn to love you more too. Plus, by telling these stories, maybe you too will realize how special your grandparents were to you.

Having trouble as you're writing? Maybe you're trying too hard. Step back a moment. Just relax and let your memory work. Have faith, pray, and try again.

"Truth is stranger than fiction, but it is because Fiction is obliged to stick to possibilities; Truth isn't."

—Mark Twain[6]

Places

Lets start another list.

This time it's places, like places you lived and places you visited that you liked. You may even want to add places you want to go, especially if there is a particular reason for that desire.

A few things you could include:

- Address
- Description
- Size (like floor plan, or 2 bed 2 bath)
- Yard and surroundings
- Neighbors / friends
- When (dates if you can)
- Why (if needed)
- Style of house (ambler, condo, townhouse, duplex, apartment)
- Memories (if not home, then where was home at that time?)

Every place you lived should have some detail. Add other places you spent a lot of time at, like friends' homes. Include whatever is relevant, and make it real.

It is important to include how the place affected you and your life and what made it home for you. If you especially loved that particular place, say so.

If you lived someplace that was really trying for you, include why. Include descriptions and details, and don't be afraid to be a little creative. Add detail that adds to the story but doesn't detract from facts.

Some of you will find this list of places to be very long. Others will have short lists. It really depends on how many places you lived. You should at least include some mention of places you lived. And just as a note, not all places are homes. One of my favorite places was the top of a tree. What place did you go for peace and quiet?

Now think. Which ones from your list do you need to add more detail to? Be visual. Can you see the setting? Will the reader be able to see the place because of your description? Use the senses: what you see, hear, smell, touch, and taste.

Your stories represent you. Make sure the readers are seeing the right person. Pull your reader into your world by using the right words.

"When a story from your life comes to mind, *that is the time to write*. It doesn't matter if you're talking about something completely different and that somehow triggers a memory of another time. If you don't have time right then, at least take a minute to make yourself a note, detailed enough to remind you."

—Janet

Technology and Inventions

Have you thought about the advances that have happened in this world since the Lord restored His Church? Many things have been brought to light to make life better for spreading the gospel, but these things affect our lives individually as well. They make a difference in our daily lives.

So today let's think about technology. Take the time to make a list of the technology in your daily life. Give yourself at least five minutes and see how long your list can get in that short time. Start by writing what you would find in homes, then maybe offices, in schools, in your pocket, and anywhere else.

Think about the technology that is behind the things you use, like your cell phone, television, computer, or tablets. Many things are in the background that affect how these things work. Think about the technology that you don't see unless you're part of that world—technology that is behind our everyday items. What about the development of these things? Do you know anyone that was involved in the creation of some big technology or invention?

What about your refrigerator, stove, microwave, or even a toaster or the hot water heater? These are all things that are new in these last few generations. Keep going. How about broadcasting general conference to us via many different devices? What is involved in that simple thing that we enjoy so much?

What was the first television like, the first computer, the first telephone, the first cell phone? What was the first one of these things *you* had? Have *you* seen them change? What do you think your grandparents would think about some of these things?

Do you remember your first television or your first computer? How did things change when this item became part of your life? What was the telephone like for you when you were young? Think about your grandparents and what they have seen in their lives. How about a refrigerator—did your grandmother have an ice box? Some of these things you may not consider as technology, so maybe we need to expand this category. How many other things affect your life that you could write about? Do you know someone who doesn't have access to some of these items? If so, what is different about their lives than yours?

What about medical technology? We have apps on our phone to track our steps or exercise. There are small specialty devices to help with diabetes and other health problems. There have also been advances to help with major surgery, like transplants, the repair of arteries and ligaments, and many others.

Whatever you decide to write about, be sure to use a lot of detail, a lot of description, and pictures if you have them. Remember, never assume that your readers know what you're talking about. For example, if I talked about my first cell phone, I would explain why I had one and include some stories of using it, but I would need to describe the cell phone itself because technology is advancing so fast that things don't stay the same very long. My first cell phone didn't look or function anything like the one currently in my pocket, and even that one is outdated.

You could write one inclusive article or story about how your life is different because of technology, or you could write several. Think about how your life would be different if suddenly a piece of technology was gone. How do you feel about life with all these inventions?

Be sure to include how these things affect your life. Think about it a minute. How do they really affect your life? Remember your first one of something? In what ways has it made your life different? How about different than your grandparents or someone older that you know well? Or even just different than when you were younger? Imagine the possibilities and what might be invented in the next fifty years.

If a story starts to form, great. Write a rough draft or at least a list of things to include. If you are like me, the stories involving these things are few, but you can create an article. Write like you're doing a newspaper article. Maybe compare your life to your grandparents' lives. Think about how you can do that. Start with the basics.

Write about these things the way they are now and how they've been in your life. That way, your descendants will have something to compare with the way things are in their lives. At the very least, your story or article could trigger gratitude for what they have.

Keep in mind that a good news article and a good story include as much as possible that fits in the categories of who, what, when, where, why, and how. You might start something like this: "My grandmother cooked on a very heavy large coal- or wood-burning stove. It also heated the house. That was quite a convenience, right there in the house. She didn't have to go outside and build a fire to cook over, or build a fire in the fireplace in the house. She had a actual stove. Of course, she still had to carry wood in from outside. As for my life, now we turn a switch and heat comes, we put a pan on it, and when it's done cooking, we turn the switch again and it's off. We don't have to carry wood, light the fire, or wait for it to heat up, and then even in summer it has to burn itself out when you're done, continuing to heat the house."

Now, what happens if we add some details, describe the stove better, or find a picture? Where in the house would the stove have been? In the kitchen? They may not have had a kitchen; most early homes didn't. Continue with descriptive language to make it interesting. Explain more of what your life is like in comparison to your grandparents. Better still, intermingle it with your story. Put it all together to make an interesting story or article. You want someone to enjoy reading it.

As you work on this, maybe you will be reminded of a story you can write. If so, add the story to what you're doing.

Think about the future. Tell it so they can visualize what you are seeing. Remember, *never* assume they know what you're talking about. It may be like you're speaking a foreign language. They haven't seen it and don't know much about it—it's new to them. Think about Isaiah when he was describing planes and trains (see Isaiah 5:28–30). He had seen it in vision, but he was writing to people who hadn't seen it. Explain and describe.

Don't be afraid to let your gratitude show through to Heavenly Father and to those on earth who made these things possible by doing their little part. If there are any emotions involved as you write, let them flow. Don't be afraid of your feelings.

“*Never* assume they know what you’re talking about.”

—Janet

“Give them details so they will be able to visualize exactly what you are talking about.”

—Janet

TRANSPORTATION

Let's think about our daily lives. What is another major item in our lives besides technology? I think it might be transportation.

How important is transportation in your life? What would change if you were suddenly on foot?

Let's start by making a list of all the means of transportation that have been part of your life: cars, trucks, motorcycles, tractors, bicycles, skateboards, horses, and so on. Maybe you started out life with a pedal car or tricycle. Where you grew up will have affected your way of getting around. Do you like to walk (or did you used to)? You could consider that transportation as well.

Be more specific about some of the things on your list. For example, list the cars you've owned, the ones your family has had, or even the ones you've loved or dreamed of having. Describe each briefly. For some, you'll want more details. Then do the same with any other means of transportation that fits your life.

As you're making these lists, notice if any specific memories are triggered. Write them down, making notes as you go. For now, no organizing, no rereading or changing, and no editing. Just write everything that pops into your head as you think about transportation. Even if it isn't on the subject, write it down. Most importantly, *allow yourself time.*

Talking or sharing helps. Let your mind wander. As the years rolled by, how did you get around? Keep adding to your list until nothing more comes to mind.

Now think about a specific story. What happened when you got your first car? Describe it in detail so well that the reader can practically see that car. What did it smell like? Include color and anything that made it different. Add any distinguishing marks, dents, or scrapes. Were the seats unique? Was there something special about it, or did it just get you from A to B and back again? Was there a particular learning experience connected with that car? Did someone else help you buy it, or did you save up for it yourself?

Keep thinking. Keep writing.

Pictures are always a good addition to true stories. If you have a photo of one of your modes of transportation, include it with the story. If not, you might be satisfied with a picture from the internet that is close. Don't use it unless you're happy with it.

In this category, I think we can all come up with at least one good story. Put it in the back of your mind as you go about your days. Make notes every time something comes to you, with enough detail to trigger your memory when you get ready to sit down and write the story or stories.

“If you don’t learn from your mistakes, what’s the use of making them?”[7]

“There is no way of writing well and also writing easily.”

—Anthony Trollope[8]

Using the Basic List

Why should you write your personal history? I could go on for days about the reasons why. However, for now I will just remind you that it is something the Lord and many of His prophets have told us to do. In this book, you will find a section on "Why?" (page 4), and as you read, many more reasons will pop up. You'll find that over the years, the *whys* will creep in.

I have created a list of things to help you remember your life. You'll find it in Part II in the section "Basic List" (page 130). As you follow the instructions, your life should begin to open up to you.

The first thing you're going to do is pick one of the things on this list. Next, you are going to make another list. Let's say you pick "favorites" from the basic list. You will now make a list of all the things that you can think of that you call your favorites. Just start writing; no order, no rereading or changing, no editing or fixing. Just write everything that pops into your head, even if it doesn't seem to be on topic. Allow yourself time, and don't try to rush.

What was the first thing you remember when you were young—something that still sticks in your mind? Did you have a favorite toy or blanket? Keep writing, adding a few details like color or something special about them. Think about now versus when you were young. Is there a difference in what you like or don't like? Have your interests changed over the years? Keep adding to the list until your mind simply stops because you just can't think of another thing.

Is there gratitude starting to swell in you for something or someplace in your world that has been important to you? Can you remember one item that had special meaning to you? Maybe you have a story about it. Write a list of things about that one item. Include things like color, style, and texture. Use descriptive words like smooth, sleek, bumpy, or shiny. Remember to add a few details or a lot if needed. Be sure to include why it was it special. Think about the story in your life that had to do with that item. Maybe it was a favorite tree. Why was it special? Write it. Just write as fast as you can think. Don't correct or change—just get the basics on paper. You are writing a rough draft of something that happened to you, or something that happened to something important to you, because of that item. For example, "My favorite tree was struck by lightning many times." Write as quickly as the thoughts come to you.

Was there an accident, like falling out of a certain tree? Or maybe something wonderful happened in a particular place. Was there a favorite sledding hill or a camping place your family enjoyed going? Why was it something you loved?

When there are no more ideas that come to mind, that marks the end of the first part. Now you can go back, adding some details, descriptions, visualizations, and feelings. Now you can organize your notes into a rough draft story. Make it come to life. Pretend you are telling this story to a child. You want them to feel like they are with you in this story, so you have to make it sing. Add details about things associated with this object or story. Did a certain car have specially made seat covers that fit your personality, or an added feature in the outside design? Maybe you share a favorite song with a special someone.

Remember to always include feelings, action words, and details. As always, don't assume they will understand if you don't explain. Feelings are especially important when your heart is involved.

Use what you've learned in the previous sections of this book, like how all stories should include who, what, when, where, why, and how. How does this relate to your treasure?

Next, put together a story. Use your rough draft. Make needed changes to polish it. Add more explanations and more visual details and set it aside for a bit until it is cold. Then reread it and see if it still sounds good or if it's missing something.

Last of all, read it to someone. The best choice is to a child, but it could be anyone. If there really isn't anyone to listen, read it aloud to yourself. That way you are using more than one sense, and you will catch things that need to be changed. Maybe you'll see things that aren't clear enough or seem a little incomplete.

“Just remember, you are valuable and your story is important. You aren’t perfect yet, and your story doesn’t need to be either.”

—Janet

What about Your Ancestors?

You may not realize it, but your ancestors have played an important role in your life, both the ones you knew and the ones you didn't know.

Think about what they did for you. What has influenced your life? What characteristics—both physical and personality traits—came from them? Do you have strengths because of their lives? Do you belong to The Church of Jesus Christ because of their actions and example? Do you wish you knew more about them?

Think about your descendants. You are, after all, *their* ancestor. What should they know about you?

Children are drawn to meaningful family stories. They enjoy learning about family culture and even (maybe especially) family recipes, and they love discovering their ancestors' experiences. Actually, they love to learn about their own parents and other people that they know. They love to hear about their parents' lives when they were their age. It gives them strength for their own lives. They like to hear stories about themselves when they were younger and even about their birth. They don't remember learning to walk or ride a bike, so tell them about these things.

Children who are connected to their ancestors are more likely to want to live righteous lives, including going to the temple.

Remember the research study we discussed? If not, go find it in Part III of this book (see page 140). By knowing where they come from, your descendants will be better in so many ways—spiritually, emotionally, and maybe even physically by being healthier.

Discover who your ancestors are. You and your family need to know about as many ancestors as possible. Start by filling out a pedigree chart as far back as you can. (You can search the internet for "pedigree chart" and print one out that way.) Add any details you can find about each one of them, even if it's only where they came from. Don't worry that you don't know as much as you wish. Let that trigger your desire to write more of your own stories. Check websites like FamilySearch—you may be surprised.

Now get to know just one of the people whose name you just wrote on your chart. Can you find enough in what you know or have? Maybe you need to do a little research. How important do you consider it to get to know them? Do you ever wonder what their lives were like? Maybe you know some of their trials but wonder about their attitudes or emotions in those situations.

Find something you will be able to cherish about them. Look for a story that has been written about them. Maybe find enough about their life that you can write a story. Dig deep enough to find your interest. Find yourself as you search.

This may take a while, but you *can* do it. Have faith in yourself and be persistent. It will be worth it.

Can we dig a little deeper? Here are some questions you might ask yourself:

- If you could have one more conversation with them, what would you ask? What would you want to tell them?
- Did this person teach you something that has changed the way you live your life? If so, be sure that is somehow incorporated into your life story.
- Is there something about them that only you may have known?
- What did you cherish most about them?
- What did you consider their special qualities and gifts to be?
- Do you have stories to tell about them that others would love to hear and pass on?

If some are still here on earth, ask them before they are gone. Find out all you can about them and those that lived before them. That information will die with them.

You may want to write a paragraph or two about each of your grandmothers, as far back as you know, and then blend them together with a little narrative that includes your thoughts and feelings. Then do the same thing with your grandfathers.

Besides making your life stories available to your family, it is important that you have copies of ancestors' stories, and be sure they are also available to your family. Work on collecting copies of journals or letters that are available, and gather copies of stories that have been written about your ancestors or others who have affected your life

For example, maybe you will find something like this. A cousin of mine wrote an article called "The Butler Murder of 1869."[9] It's about my great-grandparents, and it helps me to recognize where I got some of my strong faith. It makes me feel stronger knowing that my ancestors did some really hard things and made it through. Thus, I believe that I can too.

One of my uncles wrote about some of his experience in World War II. I also have a cousin who put together a book from letters and journals about the experiences of his father in World War II, including in a German prison camp. These two soldiers were brothers. Their stories are important to me but even more so to my descendants who are (or have been) in the military.

Collect copies of as many stories as you can, and then continue to be watchful for more stories. Get copies whenever you can. Visit the FamilySearch website to find more.

One important thing we could research for our families is who was the first in the family to join The Church of Jesus Christ of Latter-day Saints and how they came to the United States, or how they came to their religious beliefs and to the country where you currently reside.

What are some of the things you've discovered about your ancestors, or even about yourself? What are some things that you acquired from your ancestors, like hair color, a cowlick, eye color, or other features? Perhaps some traits have been passed down, like faith, spiritual strength, courage, or determination. There is no end to the possibilities. You may not find them specifically recorded, but you can figure many things out from what you do know about their lives.

Write a story about yourself that is interspersed with things you know about an ancestor. Maybe you were named for this person or you know something about them that is like you. You must have a story in your life from someone saying, "Grandma so-and-so used to do that."

Consider more about how they influenced your life, and incorporate things you learn into your own life stories. You should learn more about who you are by learning more about your ancestors. Share with your family.

"You are allowed to fail. You are allowed to start again from scratch. You are allowed to try over and over. You are allowed to struggle. No path is ever a perfectly straight line. . . . Your path is meant to wind and twist and turn in directions you never expected. It is meant to bring you unexpected highs and lows that make you stronger. You do not need to have it all figured out right now. You only need to keep taking the next step, just one at a time, because in time, you will get where you are meant to go."

—Niki Banas[10]

Share enough with your family that they will know this is true.

"Act as if what you do makes a difference. *It does.*"

—William James[11]

Do I Do Something Differently than It Was Done in the Past?

Think about what life was like a hundred or even just fifty years ago. Do you do things differently now versus then? Of course the answer is *yes*! Most of what I do is something different.

Going along with technology, think about the difference of now versus then. Consider what you do every day. Does your daily life include things that didn't exist a hundred years ago? We all know it does, but think about the specifics.

Start by making a list of things you use frequently. (See the list "Changes in the Last Hundred Years" on page 133 for some ideas.) This may include some things (probably a lot) that you have already listed with other subjects, but that's okay. Maybe it will trigger new memories. You may find it easier to go through your house, room by room. What is in that room? What do you do in that room? You could even consider if there was such a thing as that room a hundred years ago.

After you've made this list, put a star next to the things that would not have existed even fifty years ago. It may be easier to star the ones that did exist fifty years ago, since that's probably a shorter list.

How about household tools or kitchen appliances that are different? The kitchen is one area where there have been many changes. How many things can you list in the kitchen? How do those compare to what there was fifty or a hundred years ago? Do you even know how your great-grandmother cooked? Write it all down, even if you have to do a little research.

How about flooring that didn't exist—if they even had a floor? Think about the office and what is different there. Maybe you don't have an office job, but what is different where you do spend your days?

Professions are another thing to consider. For example, are you a farmer or know a farmer? How has farming changed from horses to tractors to big machinery? Consider a police officer—how did they get around? It used to be on foot or horseback, but now they are in cars, trucks, and motorcycles.

Consider your daily transportation. Again, they would have used horses earlier, maybe with a saddle, and then added buggies. Now, what do *you* use to get you around? What are some gadgets in it that hadn't even been dreamed of half a century ago?

Think about sports and other activities. Talk about what you use for recreation. Do you have a recreational vehicle? What an idea!

Think about your ancestors. What do you wish you knew about them? Now consider just two generations into the future. What might be different? What might now be part of your life that they might not understand?

Explore your world in your mind, then write about something that seems a normal part of life to you. It might be something you think isn't worth writing about or just isn't important, but you may be wrong. We tend to forget that some things we have become accustomed to really are new, even to us. Remember to use details, descriptions, and vividness. Don't leave out anything.

This subject may be better as an article. You could include how you feel about your life. Do you wish you lived a hundred years ago, or are things good for you as they are? If a story or stories come, write them down, of course.

There have been so many inventions in your lifetime. You will find some ideas in the list at the end of this book called "Changes in the Last Hundred Years." You could spend a lot of time on this subject, but don't feel like you have to.

"How do you eat
an elephant? One
bite at a time.
Write your history
the same way.
Don't look at,
or think about,
the whole thing.
One bite at
a time."

—Janet

Love Thy Neighbor

One of the big challenges in life is to look for the good in others. With some people, that's easy. It may be easy because they are so good at shining their goodness and hiding what's not so good. It may be that personalities blend or things just click. It's interesting how we feel like we know certain people when we first meet them. That feeling makes friendships far easier.

With some people, we have to work really hard to be friendly. Maybe it's just because we got off on the wrong foot with them, or maybe their personality just rubs against ours. Some people just seem to look for the unhappy side of life. Whatever the reason, we struggle to see the good in them.

We have all had both of these kinds of people in our lives. Write about one or more. Here are some questions to consider:

- How did you manage to find something good in this person?
- How did your efforts turned out?
- Did you become friends with this person?
- Did you learn to not let this person get to you?
- Are you still struggling with this person?
- Have you moved on and this person is just someone in your past?

Tell your descendants how you handled the situation and how it made you a better person. They will undoubtedly face the same situation.

Remember to write a story, not a documentary, if possible. Story doesn't necessarily mean the typical story—this happened, that happened, and we all lived happily ever after. By *story* I just mean include details and bring it to life. Don't leave the reader feeling like they just read a lecture or discussion. Bring them into the situation in some way so they can feel how you felt and learn from it what you did.

"When Mormon saw that his Nephite people were about to be exterminated, he set out to 'write a small abridgment' of their records. This project began at the last location where the Nephites camped before they finally gathered to the land of Cumorah. The subsistence conditions the Nephites were enduring could not have been anything but harsh; the people were refugees with uncertain sources of food, clothing, and shelter. Mormon's writing activity probably extended into the four-year period of preparation for the final battle agreed to by the Lamanite commander, but in any case the abridged history was completed and the archive was buried in the Hill Cumorah well before the final conflict."

—Professor John L. Sorensen[12]

Now, do you think things are too difficult or too challenging to take the time to write? I have to admit that sometimes I do, but we shouldn't—we really have it pretty easy. Let's share our goods and bads with future generations. After all, we survived an earthquake on top of the COVID-19 virus and more.

Oh, how blessed we are!

“One day, the story you write of how you overcame what you went through will be someone’s survival guide as they face their storms.”

—Janet

Writing Your Stories

There is only one wrong way to write your personal history: to not write it at all. That said, let's cover some things that might make your stories more enjoyable to read.

Think about a garden. You have a friend who is blind and you want him or her to see the beauty of all the hard work you have put into your garden.

It is late August, so harvest season is upon us. You have planted lots of varieties of vegetables, plus a lot of different kinds of flowers. Now think about how you are going to describe your garden so your friend can enjoy it. Let's just think about a few possibilities.

Remember to use descriptive words. (Refer to the "Adjectives" list on page 138 if needed.) Use your five senses and your imagination. For example, here is how I might describe things.

The tomato plants are bright green foliage with luscious, plump tomatoes in a variety of red tones, depending on the ripeness. Close your eyes and imagine yourself picking one off the vine. As you take a big bite, feel the juice running down your chin. So delicious.

We like cucumbers—do you? The vines spread all around. There are big, beautiful green leaves, fuzzy stickers on the back, and the stems are prickly. If you feel them, it will help you to get the picture better. All I see is vines, but as I move them a little, I find beautiful long cucumbers that were hiding by being the same color among the vines. They look so yummy to me that I think we need to try one. I'll just wipe the dirt off on my pants, take out a pocket knife, and cut off a piece. Can you hear how crisp it is? Now notice the crunchy, fresh taste.

Oh, and over here are peppers. There's a whole row of different kinds. The leaves are kind of a dull green, but each bush has a different color and shape of peppers. There are shiny, long red ones and a whole bunch of orange ones. This bush of yellow ones is really loaded. Over here are three bushes of sweet cooking peppers. There is a bush of some dull yellow ones, but they are the hot ones. The bell peppers are bigger—not long but more round. Here's a bush of sparkling red ones and a bush of shimmering green ones and orange ones too.

Now, the corn looks totally different than anything else in the garden. Everything else is lying on the ground, but the corn stretches for the sky. Strong, straight stalks rise above our heads. On each one is a dull greenish-yellow thing that's called an ear, looking somewhat like two canoes, one regular and the second upside down on top of it. Or maybe two gravy boats is a better description—depends on what you're most familiar with. It really doesn't look appetizing, but if we pull one off the stalk, put it in a fire or grill, and then open it up, there will be a beautiful yellow cob full of juicy corn, which of course we cover in butter and a little salt and pepper. Bite into that and taste the heaven of fresh corn on the cob.

Well, I don't know about you, but I'm getting hungry!

Begin to see how you can use adjectives to bring your story to life. You are only limited by your imagination. Let it run wild.

"When you feel like you're drowning in life, remember, your lifeguard walks on water."[13]

"Your writings can be magical when your words touch the heart of your reader."

—Janet

Scripture Stories

Heavenly Father wants all of His children home again, "in families and in glory."[14] Imagine your unique role in that plan. Think about your descendants who also have a unique part in the plan.

Nephi describes his family discovery experience: "And thus my father . . . did discover the genealogy of his fathers. . . . And now when my father saw all these things, he was filled with the Spirit" (1 Nephi 5:16–17). At that moment of discovery, Lehi was filled with the Spirit and his heart was turned to his fathers. He was excited to know about his ancestors, and he and his family were able to hold fast to the Lord's path because they had stories of their ancestors.

Do you enjoy discovering things? Learning about our lives through stories, photos, and other memories, along with the names, dates, and places we find, can be a great discovery for us and our families.

Children love to learn about their ancestors. Children resonate with meaningful family stories, and they love discovery experiences.

You do not know what from your life might help one of your descendants to hold fast to truth and righteousness. So write your stories. Use the scriptures as an influence and reminder of how important it is to write. Record your stories and all the stories you know about your ancestors. Make sure your spiritual strengths shine. Include some of your weaknesses—they need to know you weren't perfect. They need to be able to say, "My grandparents made it through hard times, and *I can too*."

So continue to think about the scriptures and the stories you read in them. Do you have some favorites? We all do. Do you have one very favorite?

Start by making a list of all the scripture stories that are meaningful to you. Then write just a little about why it is meaningful to you for each one you listed. Why it is one of your favorites? As you're doing this, did your mind go to a story, a trial in your life, or just a difficult time when scriptures helped you maneuver your way through? Write about it. Maybe even when you were feeling down or unloved and the scriptures got you back up. Is there a particular story that helps you stay on the path of righteousness?

You may want to start a story with something like this: "While reading this scripture, I remembered a time it helped me . . ." Let your descendants know how the scriptures have helped you through trials, or just how they have kept you strong. Maybe you got the rejuvenation you needed when you were discouraged or feeling alone. Write about it.

Delve into your innermost self. How has the Lord made a difference in your life? Share one of your million stories. You might consider including some quotes from the scriptures—just a few. Include ways these stories have helped you be better or hold fast through trials. Be specific: "This scripture helped me with this trial." Use it as part of a story.

What would your life be missing if that scripture story wasn't there, or if you didn't have these scriptures to turn to for strength? Perhaps your success through a trial will help a precious family member make it through theirs, even long after you are on the other side of the veil. What will your descendants be missing if *your* life stories aren't there?

Be sure to include your feelings and love for the scriptures, but be careful that you don't make it sound like a lecture. You're not telling them what they should do, just what worked for you.

Stories from the Restoration or Your Ancestors

Can you think of a story from the Restoration that has strengthened your testimony? Or a story from your family's background?

Have you heard stories from the early years of the still ongoing Restoration that have strengthened your faith, your courage, or even your belief in yourself? Have you said to yourself, "If they could do that, I can do what I need to do"?

One that brings a lump to my throat is the image of Emma Smith escaping persecution in Missouri with her four children while her husband was unjustly imprisoned in Liberty Jail. With an eight-year-old holding one side of her skirt and a six-year-old on the other side, a two-year-old in one arm and an infant in the other, and the only copy of some translation Joseph had done of the Bible safely tucked in bags that had been sewn and buttoned under her skirt, she began a faith-filled trek across the thinly frozen Missouri River.

Can you envision her walking very carefully, praying every step that she wouldn't fall through the thin ice? Those large skirts had to be challenging to walk in during winter just by themselves—now just imagine adding to it snow, ice, and a river that's lurking dangerously below, threatening your every step to become your last. Plus, with every breath you're conscious of the lives of your four precious children and the non-replaceable papers you carry beneath your skirt. Can you take a deep breath of cold air and feel just a touch of her anxiety in spite of her faith, which had to be amazing?

Can you see how important details are? What if someone just wrote, "Emma crossed the Missouri River with the translation and four children"? Would that touch your heart? Could you gain strength from such an emotionless statement? There is a marvelous painting of this scene by David Green that would be worth looking up to help your imaginings.[15]

When you heard that story, did you wonder if *you* would be able to do that? Did it give you added courage to do what you need to do?

As I think of this story and so many others, I think of their emotions. What were they going through in addition to the physical challenges? What emotions do these stories stir in you that come from your own stories? What if no one had written these stories and the stories in the scriptures? What would your life be missing? What about your stories, your faith, your courage, your determination, and your sacrifice? Perhaps you can remember times in your life when you faced a challenge with faith in God and just moved forward, one foot in front of the other, until the Lord said, "That is enough."

Think back on your life. Maybe you're going to say that nothing spectacular has happened to you. But you're just so close to it that you can't see it. Look a little deeper, then write a simple story from your life. Maybe it's one you don't think is that important, but you can see God's hand in it. You don't see what God knows. Remember too that the Lord knows who and what will come and what stories from your life could help your descendents. He can't get your stories into the hands of those who need them if you don't write them. Do you think Nephi was conceited for writing his stories? Neither are you if you write it like it was and is. Let go of your self-consciousness and write.

Just write from your life. If you include your feelings and enough details, I promise that your faith, courage, and strengths will come out where needed to help someone through their trials and hard days.

You will show that when you need to do something for what you believe, you just move forward, one step at a time, even if you don't realize you're doing it. Details bring life and emotions to stories.

What if no one writes the stories that will strengthen those you love, like the stories that lift and strengthen you? You must write yours for the coming generations. Write for you too; you need to know how good the Lord knows you are. You might gain courage for your future by recognizing it in your past.

"Life without God is like an unsharpened pencil—it has no point."

—Billy Graham[16]

The World around You

What do you see when you take time to be observant? You've heard the old saying, "Stop and smell the roses," haven't you? Growing up, did you spend a lot of time outdoors, or did you stay in most of the time?

You may want to start this by making a list of what is in your world. What do you see when you're being observant? There is a list in Part II called "The World Around You" if you'd like to use it (see page 136). Add or subtract from it to get your list.

Here are some questions you might ask yourself to help trigger a story:

- What do you see around you right now?
- What have you seen in this beautiful world?
- Did your parents take you places where you saw the beauty of the world?
- Were you one who loved to lie in the grass and watch the clouds? What things could you see there?
- Did lightning intrigue you or frighten you?
- Is it fun to watch a storm roll across the sky?
- Do you love to look at the stars?
- Have you dreamed of the beauties you'll see when you go for a hike?
- Do you particularly notice flowers or trees?
- Were you privileged to live in the country and could watch the crops grow?
- Have you enjoyed the sights, smells, and tastes of a garden?
- Is there something else that sparks in you a love of nature?

You may want to discuss some of these things with family. Get their point of view. What did they see in that mountain climb or camping trip?

Find something that you remember. Use your senses and lots of adjectives (see the "Adjectives" list on page 138) to build your vivid story for others to see, smell, taste, and touch what you did.

"We can serve by enduring well, for our steadiness will steady others who are otherwise on the verge of giving up."

—Shanon Brooks[17]

Who would you rather steady than you own family? Do it by writing your stories.

MEDICAL

This one may take some time, but it won't take any emotions or terrible effort on your part. It's probably not a story or even an article, just a collections of records, but it is important. This topic is medical records.

I suspect you have all been asked a question like, "Have any of your family members had cancer, heart trouble, an auto-immune disease, or other chronic health problems?" Did you know the answer? Would it have helped in your healthcare somehow if you had?

So, what you need to do is collect your medical records. All you really need is a list of diagnoses. Some may need a little detail, but even just a simple list would be very helpful to your descendants.

Whether you add a story or not, it is important to collect your medical information. It could actually save a life. Now, don't you think that would be worth the trouble?

If you've been seeing the same doctor a long time, this will be easy. He or she will have the records from their own office as well as from specialists that you've seen.

Research. Record. Review. Remember. Talk to the medical staff or someone who can help you gather this information. Length doesn't matter.

You may not have any stories in this area, *but* maybe you do. Sometimes health problems bring about a lot of growth and stories. This is where the emotions could come in. If you do have a story, write like always, including details such as symptoms and explanations. Make sure your reader knows what problems this health situation created, especially if it is or could be hereditary.

Short or long doesn't matter—just be sure it includes everything they may need. Think about what you could have used from your family.

"If we teach by the Spirit and you listen by the Spirit, some one of us will touch on your circumstance, sending a personal prophetic epistle just to you."

—Elder Jeffrey R. Holland[18]

When you listen to general conference, think about your life and your descendants. What does the Lord want you to tell them? The Lord may touch your heart in more than one way. I challenge you to write what comes to you.

Occasions, Food, and Gratitude

I believe that most of our food memories are associated with occasions of some sort, so I'd like to combine the two here. That doesn't mean you can't write about one without the other—of course you can. I'm also going to add gratitude in this section.

Some of my food memories have to do with simple family meals together around the dinner table. Sometimes it was more than just our family, but a lot of times we just enjoyed each other's company around a really good home-cooked meal. I am grateful my mother was a very good cook and that she taught me how to cook as well.

Other memories relate to times like Thanksgiving, Christmas, birthdays, or family reunions. There was always food and fun. So think about your memories. I hope you have some really good memories that fit these categories.

Let's start by developing a general list of occasions, then think about what kinds of things would need to be included under each occasion. Do you have traditional foods for your holiday meals? Can someone in your family mention a certain food that would start your mouth watering? Maybe there are foods that come from your ancestors that you remember, like Danish rice pudding, English trifle, or Irish stew. There is bound to be something. Maybe you don't even know where some of your traditional foods came from. Definitely include a recipe if you have one. If you need to do a little research, do it. A list of your favorite foods might help trigger a story.

Did your mother bake bread? Does the smell of bread (even passing a bakery) trigger memories? What other food smells bring back memories of years past? Smells are powerful memory triggers. How often have you said when you walked into a room, "Something sure smells good"? Think about some of those memories. Is there a story? Maybe there isn't anything particular to write a story about and you just want to write about Thanksgivings in general and what they meant to you. Maybe Christmas would bring back something. Was there a special birthday you remember? Do memories of holidays as a child fill your heart with gratitude for your family, for your life, and for those you love and cherish?

Maybe you are like so many of us as we travel through life—we just don't pay enough attention to the little things that bring us joy. Here is a story I read years ago. It comes from an old parable adapted over many generations, and it reminds us to be grateful for what we have right now.

> An American businessman was at the pier of a small coastal Mexican village when a small boat with just one fisherman docked. Inside the small boat were several large yellowfin tuna. The American complimented the Mexican on the quality of his fish and asked how long it took him to catch them.
>
> "Only a little while," the Mexican replied.
>
> The American businessman then asked, "Well, why don't you stay out longer and catch more fish?"
>
> "I have enough fish to support my family. That's all I need," the Mexican fisherman simply responded.
>
> The American was confused. "What do you do with the rest of your time?" he asked.
>
> The Mexican fisherman didn't have to think. "I sleep late, fish a little, play with my children, take siestas with my wife Maria, stroll into the village each evening where I sip wine and play guitar with my amigos. I have a full and busy life."
>
> The American businessman was quiet for a while, still confused. "I am a Harvard MBA and can help you," he started. "Seeing the way you fish, I think you should spend more time fishing so you can afford a bigger boat. With a bigger boat, you'll be able to catch more fish. With the money that more fish bring, you'll be able to buy several boats, hire more people, and make more profit. Eventually, you would have a whole fleet of fishing boats. Instead of selling your catch to a buyer, you can become a wholesaler, eventually opening your own cannery. You would control the product, processing, and distribution and reap all the financial benefits. You would need to leave this small coastal fishing village, of course, as it's too small. Somewhere like Mexico City, LA, or New York would be a much better fit. These places will help you grow your expanding enterprise."
>
> After he'd finished, the Mexican fisherman asked, "But how long will this take?"
>
> To which the American businessman replied, "About 15–20 years."
>
> "And what then?" asked the Mexican.
>
> That's when the American laughed, chuffed with the opportunity to dazzle the curious fisherman. "That's the best part. When the time comes, you can sell your company and become a very, very rich man. You would make millions!"
>
> "Millions—then what?"

> The American was slightly taken aback. "Then you could retire, of course. You could move to a small coastal fishing village where you could sleep late, fish a little, play with your kids, take siestas with your wife Maria, stroll to the village in the evenings, sip wine, and play your guitar with your amigos."[19]

Which one of them do you think was grateful for what he already had? Do we see others' trials and hardships and realize how blessed we are, or do we just look at what we think is missing in our lives and feel sorry for ourselves?

Let's make a list of things we are grateful for. Give yourself five minutes to write. As always, remember that if your mind wanders to something not on the subject, write it down. Always write whatever you think of. Now go and build your list. You may not have a story for this, and maybe one will come later. Just be sure you have your list. Follow by writing a paragraph for each one. If your category was too general, that's alright—just write a long paragraph or more than one. Everything you are grateful for should be worthy of at least a sentence. Even if you never write a story, keep your gratitude list as part of your history and update it regularly.

These three lists may get all mixed up, and that's perfectly acceptable. Just be sure that someplace, somehow, you have lists containing occasions, food, and gratitude *and* information, details, and descriptions about each. Your five senses should be very helpful with this one. We are all different, but sharing sometimes helps us remember. So if you do this as a group, be sure to share.

Because we are all different, it is essential to explain our traditions. My husband and I didn't celebrate occasions much after the children were grown. We just did things for each other when the thought came. He brought me flowers frequently, but occasions often went unnoticed by both of us. Other people put great stock in occasions, making them a priority, so our writings about this subject will be very different. What will yours be like?

Food is certainly not something we all have in common. Our favorites, our tastes, and our traditions are all very different. When you write about foods, do your best to describe smells and looks. When I mentioned Thanksgiving pudding, my brother said his mouth started watering. What memories are vivid to your taste?

You decide if these three go together or separate. For me, they are separate but they *do* overlap a lot. You do what works best for you. These topics are important.

“Look up
at the stars
and *believe*
that something
wonderful
is going
to happen.”

—Janet

“I’m not interested in whether you’ve stood with the great; I’m interested in whether you’ve sat with the broken.”

—Sue Fitzmaurice[20]

Diamonds and Pencils

What do diamonds and pencil lead have in common? They both start the same way! Carbon is the common denominator.

Pencil lead is carbon that is pressed and sticks together. As it's used, tiny bits of carbon or graphite come off and make marks.

Diamonds are carbon that has been under a lot of pressure for a long time. It's been banged and chipped until it becomes a precious stone in the rough. Finally, after it has been dug and banged around some more to get it out of the ground, it is cut or ground and eventually becomes a beautiful gem of great value.

In your stories, write about how you became a diamond. You *are* a diamond, you know. Yes, maybe you're not finished, not perfect *yet*—we won't become perfect in this life—but you are a diamond, and you have had a lot of pressures, bumps, and chips along the way that have made you what you are so far. The Lord still has some cutting, grinding, and polishing to do before you're finished, but in the experiences that have brought you to this point, there has been a lot of growing, and there's a lot that can help others in their struggles through life. That is partially why you are writing your stories.

Write about something along the path that has contributed to your growth. Maybe it's a trial or set of trials and how they helped build you into what you are today. Maybe it's just life experiences that have been character-building, even if they weren't serious trials. You've come a long way. Your descendants are going to have a rough life and will need your help, and it will help them if they know how you made it through. Help them believe they can have the strength to keep going and keep trying when the pressure seems too much.

Be sure to weave your spiritual strength into your stories. Let them know who you are. Include feelings and maybe some sights and smells.

Don't leave out your failings. Not everything in life works out the way we hoped, and it won't for our descendants either. If they know that you had times you didn't succeed, they may gain some strength when they have failings. Be sure to include how you handled the problem. Was it something you needed to try again with to eventually succeed, or was it something you needed to let go and just learn from? Remember what Thomas Edison said: "I have not failed. I've just found 10,000 ways that won't work."[21]

"Life isn't about waiting for the storm to pass. It's about learning to dance in the rain."

—Vivian Greene[22]

See what's amazing all around you.

See the Amazement

Be amazed at life around you. How we see the world around us shows in our lives, and since we are writing about our lives, it shows in our stories.

Do you ever think about the grandness of our Father's creations? Is it an opportunity for amazement?

Have you ever watched the Hubble Space Telescope? Think about just what we know about our world—we really know so very little. Isn't it amazing what we are blessed with? As we recognize God's love and power, we can become more grateful.

Have you considered the galaxy our earth is part of? We are actually here, on a planet created specifically for us. Our globe is situated so perfectly that we have enough oxygen to keep us alive, enough water to keep us going, enough gravity to keep us in place, but not too much of anything. We are here, at exactly the right spot in a whirlpool of stars, alive and conscious, walking and talking on a big rock circling in a perfect orbit that keeps going.

No matter how you look at it, this world the Lord created for us is amazing. We need to recognize that and look at our lives with a little wonder, being more aware of the beauties of this amazing world.

Take time to notice the beauties around you, and let it enhance your stories.

Part of a talk by Elder Richard G. Scott gives us a religious perspective on this and a very good demonstration of the power of using the right words:

> Recently I stood on the north shore of a beautiful Pacific island gazing out to sea at daybreak. I was fascinated by the regularity with which the gigantic waves consistently moved forward to break on the shoreline. It reminded me of the constancy of the plan of the Lord, with its fixed, eternal law, and the security of enduring justice and the tenderness of mercy when earned by obedience. I noticed that each wave would crest at a different point on the horizon to find its unique path to shore. Some cascaded over rocks, leaving rivulets of foaming, white water. Others burst on the shore in individual patterns. They slid up the moistened sand with playful frothy edges, then bubbled and swirled as they receded. . . .
>
> Since there would be no further opportunity to observe the majestic sea, I tried to imagine the glorious panorama the brilliant sun would later create. As I watched this magnificent scene in reverence, a window formed in the clouds; the glistening rays of the rising sun broke through the overcast sky, transforming everything with its luminescence, its color,

> its life. It was as if the Lord wanted to share an additional blessing, a symbol of the light of His teachings that gives brilliance and hope to everyone it touches. Tears of gratitude formed for this wondrous world in which we live, for the extraordinary beauty our Heavenly Father so freely shares with all who are willing to see. Truly, life is beautiful. . . .
>
> Do you take time to discover each day how beautiful your life can be? How long has it been since you watched the sun set? The departing rays kissing the clouds, trees, hills, and lowlands good night, sometimes tranquilly, sometimes with exuberant bursts of color and form. What of the wonder of a cloudless night when the Lord unveils the marvels of His heavens—the twinkling stars, the moonlight rays—to ignite our imagination with His greatness and glory?[23]

Notice how he weaves his faith into the story but uses marvelous descriptions to help us envision what he is seeing. When you write, describe what you see in such a way that a child will ask questions about it and will want to know more about you and your life.

Opportunities for amazement are all around us. Let the delight and awe come through like a little child who for the first time sees a butterfly or tastes ice cream and says with wide-eyed wonder, "What *is* it?"

Allow the gratitude and "wow" in your life to show in your writing—the wonders of little things discovered. See with the eyes of a child where the simplest things are amazing: a blade of grass, being licked by a puppy, riding piggyback on your daddy.

Have you ever thought about the miracle of being able to run your eyes over a bunch of black crooked lines on a white page and have it fill your mind with tales of dragons and heroes and fairy godmothers, or far-away lands you didn't know existed?

And just as others are amazing to you, you are also amazing to them.

Perhaps if we look at life with amazement more often, we will be able to convey our thoughts and feelings to our families in a way that will help them have better, stronger, more faith-filled lives—and *that* is why we write.

Now pull yourself into at least one amazing time in your life and write about it using enough descriptive words to bring your reader right into your story. Make them feel they are right there, wanting to read more and more.

Share a simple beauty in your life, perhaps something no one else noticed. Have you ever been overwhelmed with wonder? Bring it to life. Make it real to the reader. Bring it into a story that will fill descendants with amazement. If it's a place, make them want to see it. If you truly put yourself there, it will be easier to write about it. Describe why and how it affects you.

Explain your amazement in your story. This one will need lots of emotion and the right words.

Remember to use descriptions that enhance your stories. We always talk about adjectives. They are particularly important for these stories.

"It's not how much we give but how much love we put into giving."

—Mother Teresa[24]

So be sure you put a lot of love into your stories. They will need it!

"Keep going, and don't worry about your speed. You're making progress, even if it doesn't seem like it. Forward is forward, no matter how slow."

—Lori Deschene[25]

Our Heritage

We all have a valuable heritage. What we do with it affects our lives. Some people grow and learn as they accept the talents and strengths they inherited, while others, to use a well known phrase, "die with their music still in them."

I know of a special young woman who has so much potential, but as a child she was abused and she can't seem to get past that—she can't love herself. A wonderful young man loves her, and they were married for a few years, but she just couldn't get past her childhood and left her potential unused. He and his family did all they could to help her know she was loved. I'm convinced she also had grandmothers in heaven trying to help her.

I also know many who have accepted their responsibilities and honored their heritage by making their own music. So today you need to write about your heritage. Write about your grandmothers and grandfathers, back as far as you know anything. What did you inherit from them? What do you hope to gain from them? Share just a touch of their story. Write about how their stories have affected you. You could include some of what you have done with the traits you inherited. Maybe you need to include how you feel about them.

If there is something in your past, or some trait you inherited, that wasn't really good, you can learn from that also. Maybe lightly mention this point and what you have learned. Maybe you simply learned not to be that way.

I have family members that are nervous worriers. I determined when I was young that I wouldn't be that way, but it hasn't always been easy. Knowing that tendency is there helps me to avoid it. The same applies to good things. Knowing that your grandmother had amazing faith can help you to believe you can have strong faith too.

Have you ever really thought about how much your ancestors influence your life? How are you going to find out what you got from them?

Start with what you know. Dig deep in your memory—relax and remember. Do you remember hearing stories told by parents or grandparents? Maybe even a favorite uncle or aunt told some stories. Maybe you have some revealing records. Where are they?

Talk to living family to learn all you can. Find out what they know. Do they have any written stories or even verbal ones they can share? Pictures would be great.

The next step is to use FamilySearch. You may be surprised what you find. I hope it's lots and that all your surprises are pleasant ones.

You may notice there are some things you wish you knew. Maybe you can mention it. Whether you share or not, make sure you use it as a reminder of things you need to include from your life for your future readers.

I have a grandmother who was attacked by a man and left for dead. Reading her story, I see her faith in God, her faith in the power of the priesthood, and her faith in her husband. So I know those strengths are in me if I will just use them.

Find all the stories you can of your ancestors, including your own parents. Keep a copy, and record what you've learned about your own inner strengths and how you feel about them.

In addition to making your life stories available to your family, it is important that you have copies of your ancestors' stories, and be sure they are available for any interested family members. If you know stories that aren't written, *you* write them. Ancestors' stories, especially our parents' stories, tell us a lot about who we are.

Spend a little time here and there, now and then, on collecting copies: copies of journals, letters, stories, documents, anything that is available. Also collect copies of stories others have written that are about your ancestors or have affected your life. I am grateful for anything I can get a hold of. I really appreciate others' efforts in researching and compiling stories of my ancestors.

Every story that I read about others' struggles—whether about my ancestors or others—lifts and strengthens me. I am a better person because someone left a record.

I have read stories of military service in my family, which strengthens my patriotic feelings and my gratitude for the freedom I enjoy. They bless my life.

There are also ancestors who left comfortable lives to go, under difficult circumstances, to another land where they hoped they could have religious freedom. I want copies of their stories. Their lives have greatly affected my life and who I am. If those stories don't exist, I need to do some research, add it to what I know, and write the stories. You also have that need. It's not easy, but it's doable. We also need to remember the Lord's timetable and pray about where we need to focus our current efforts.

What stories do you already have copies of? This section may be more for your growth right now, *but* your descendants will also have these stories that you collect and will gain strength from them as well. Plus, part of this section is to write about the feelings you've had when you've learned about your ancestors. Or you may want to write about what you feel influenced your life.

If this seems like a daunting task, that's because it is. However, you don't have to do it all at once. I promise you that it's worth every effort and the necessary learning, time, and creativity. Plus, it can be fun to discover stories of your ancestors as you continue to discover your own stories. You will also discover more about who you are. Gather stories from people who know those stories, before those people are gone. Life is fleeting, and this is important. There may not be a lot you can do in this area now, but at least talk to those you know and record the stories they know. Do it soon.

I am fully aware that for some of you, this is impossible—there simply are no records. Instead of letting this discourage you in your search, allow this fact to encourage you to write. Whatever you find, whatever you do, don't get discouraged—just do all you can. You are a valuable person. Your life has worth. Record it. Someday, someone will be so grateful you did.

My ancestors came from Denmark, Scotland, England, and Ireland. I can leave for my family their names and a few basic details about where they came from. I can also learn traits that are typical of these countries and wonder if I have those traits. Where do your ancestors come from? Are you primarily one nationality or from dozens? One important thing we could record, if we know it, is how they came to join The Church of Jesus Christ of Latter-day Saints and how they came to the United States. Those stories will be fascinating. If those things don't apply to you, there may be something about religious freedom or at least about the country your ancestors lived in that will be interesting. How these things came to be tells a lot about their strengths and fortitude.

So, what are you going to do? How are you going to start? Where are you going to look for information? I really wish I knew more about how to find stories. I have shared all I know, for now at least. Occasionally you will find something by just typing the ancestor's name into a Google search. As you discover stories, maybe you can share how you found them and thus help us all find ours. We are all still learning.

As you collect your stories, it would be a good idea to record how you feel as you search and also how you feel when you find something.

"Every death is like the burning of a library."

—Alex Haley[26]

Don't allow this to be true when you leave this life. Leave your written stories.

Why write your history? Elder D. Todd Christofferson said the following:

Part of the reason we focus on history is that the Lord has commanded it. He made that a commandment in the very first day the Church was organized, to keep a record. Part of it is to honor those who have gone before but also to take courage from their example. Remember them, as Prophet Brigham Young said, that battalion members would be remembered through all generations, and that memory inspires us. We see what others have done; we say: "I can do that. Others have, I can, too."

But it also shows the hand of God all the way through our history, and I think that's tremendously important for building faith. He's been there from the beginning. He's been there all along. He's with us. And He never abandons His people, whatever their trials or challenges. So remembering the past, the history teaches us lessons about what to do, about how to do it, and inspires us; but more than anything else, it teaches us that God is with us.[27]

Write an Article

Lets do something different today. Let's write an article. Now, you may wonder what that has to do with your history. Well, there are things in your life that your descendants may wonder about, or maybe they won't wonder but will be surprised when they read about it. These things really don't lend to a story, but they're worth recording.

For example, write about the clothes you have worn through your life, how styles have changed, and how what you like has changed.

You could write about the political scene. Were you involved? If so, to what extent? What has changed with different presidents, different mayors, or other civic leaders? How have politics affected your life?

You could write about something you're passionate about, something you would want others to know. Maybe it's even something you don't want anyone to know while you're alive but think it would be good for after you're gone. Let your mood run wild, then put it on paper. Write it like a news article *or* a research paper.

Make it interesting and informative. Dates and places may be helpful.

It may help to think about something your ancestors probably did daily that you wonder about. Wash day is a good one. The way your ancestors did their washing, the way I did it, and the way you do it are probably three very different things.

You still need to include feelings, and emotions would especially come out if you write about something you're passionate about. My family's involvement in the military and my patriotic spirit are the subject of my first article. Find something you truly believe in but don't have a story for. Like always, create a list of the things you want to include, add how they affect you, and put it into an article they will enjoy. Think about news articles you have read. What makes some of them so interesting that you read the whole thing, while others are so boring that you either just start of just skim? Articles have a basic rule: think who, what, when, where, why, and how.

"If there is a Goliath in front of you, there must be a David inside of you."[28]

You really are better than you think you are.

Trials: Experiences We've Grown From

Our goal here on earth is to one day return to live with our Father in Heaven with our family. So, if by writing our stories we can help our family to make it through their trials, then don't you think it's important that we tell them about *our* trials and how *we* made it through? I promise that it will help someone.

Think about something that was a big trial in your life, or even one that wasn't so big. Just start this when the memory comes. Remember the details, and start making a list of things to include when you put it together. Be sure to include as much description as needed to help them see. Explain how it started, how it ended, and how you grew in the process. Was is sudden or gradual? Did you know from the beginning, or did it hit you later?

This story is one you may not wish to share in this life—it's your choice. But you definitely should leave it in your history for the future. Write it whether you plan to share it now or not.

As you're thinking of a challenging time, a trial in your life, remember the details: your struggle, your prayers, the miracles that might have been plentiful, the inspiration that helped you know what to do to make it through, and what you learned from this experience. Take a lot of time—don't rush. Let your feeling come through. Include all the emotions you remember feeling. Include enough detail that you put your readers in the story and they become part of it. They will be able to grow from your trouble without having to physically go through it themselves. You just shared a strength.

Sometimes it helps to use thoughts or statements from someone else to better express how we really feel. This is fine. Give credit and explain why you used it. For example, here's a statement from a new member of the Church to the missionaries who taught him: "I really don't mind going through so much stuff. If Jesus did all that for me, it doesn't make sense that I don't have to take a little suffering too."

Sometimes we find it difficult to express our feelings in writing. It is hard to decide if we even want to share this story, and if we do, what parts to share and how. Pray a lot, and let God help you. This story will help someone you will love. Be sure to give them an extra chance to handle their challenges.

Emotions are a big part of trials. Be sure to include them. Don't leave out all the depression, discouragement, or even anger. Did you talk to yourself a lot about not letting this get you down? How did you hang on? Did you feel alone? Did you have support from family or friends? Always point out that the Lord was there, as long as you would accept Him. Let your spiritual strength come out. Don't hide it. And allow some weaknesses also. Don't try to be too humble. You can always use the scriptures as a guide. There you can find many trials and the strengths they used to deal with those hard times.

So, decide which trial or hard time you want to start writing about. Now go!

Again, this story is one you may not wish to share in this life, but you need to leave it in your history for the future. Write it whether you plan to share it now or not. You are also writing for you. By writing and letting it all come out on paper, you can find peace where there may still be pain.

"In the gospel of Jesus Christ you have help from both sides of the veil, and you must never forget that. When disappointment and discouragement strike—and they will—you must remember and never forget that if our eyes could be opened we would see horses and chariots of fire as far as the eye can see riding at reckless speed to come to our protection."

—Elder Jeffrey R. Holland[29]

More Tips for Using the Basic List

In Part II of this book, on page 130, you will find the "Basic List." I mentioned this in an earlier chapter. Pick a subject from that list, then make a list of things that fit in that subject and fit your life.

For example, let's say you pick animals. List every pet you ever owned, played with, or loved. Now pick one of those. Get hold of a story that comes out of it. Make a list of everything you can think of about that story. From this, you will write your story.

How do you write a good story? Write a rough draft of the story as you remember it, beginning to end. Then go back through it and add details. Take notice of little things that will bring the scene to life. Put your reader in the setting.

Add feelings and thoughts you had at the time and later. There may have been some emotions involved. If so, explain them. Emotions can be difficult to explain, but they're very important.

Was there a spiritual lesson or testimony-building side to it? If applicable, add details about your desires, struggles, and triumphs.

Success equals using as much as you can of the following:

- Who, what, when, where, why, and how
- Senses: hear, see, smell, taste, feel
- Possible ingredients: truth, humor, romance, your love
- Explain, describe, infuse with emotion
- Time, memories

Be prayerful. You are writing a sacred document.

Choose wisely what will be included, but first write everything you think of. Later choose if something needs to be added or deleted. Make these decisions through inspiration. Talk to the Lord—He is the only one who knows what will be good in years to come. Ask Him.

If you don't get a clear answer to delete something, *leave it in.*

"A meaningful life is not about being rich, being popular, being highly educated, or being perfect. It is about being real, being humble, being strong, and being able to share ourselves and touch the lives of others."[30]

"I urge you, with all the hope of my heart, to pray to understand your spiritual gifts—to cultivate, use, and expand them, even more than you ever have. You will change the world as you do so."

—Russell M. Nelson[31]

And you will change your descendants as you share your growth and recognition with them—your story of how you did it.

Still More Ways to Write

If you're having a hard time getting your thoughts down, consider these other ways you can write.

Poetry

There are many of you out there who have poetry in your blood. If so, you may wish to write at least some of your stories as poems or rhyme.

I can't teach you how to write a poem, but there are a couple of examples in Part III of this book, "Stories by Students and Other Writings."

Write from the Viewpoint of an Inanimate Object

We have talked about ways to write a story. We also discussed writing an article in some cases instead of or in addition to a story.

Today I want to discuss another way to write: writing from the point of view of an inanimate object. I have used this several times and it works really well for some stories. It may sound funny, but let's think about it.

Objects in our lives can see things we can't or don't want to see. For example, think about a briefcase, a car, or any of the things you may have on your list of things in life. What things would be in a place to "see" the goings on in your life?

Actually, the two I have used this for are not about me, but they give a different perspective on the story.

This can be a way to include stories that are hard to share but ought to be in your history—things that you may be uncomfortable talking about. You can include feelings that are hard to share, like this:

- "I believe he thinks . . ."
- "He seems to feel . . ."
- "There is fear in his face."
- "They're laughing."
- "I see sorrow behind her smile."
- "Her laughter covers her pain."

Use this as a way to include your physical appearance without feeling vain. For example, the mirror on the wall can share how you thought someone else felt, maybe about something you said. You can even scold yourself for things you should not have said or thought, hoping your family will learn from your errors.

Include what expressions might have been on people's faces, or how their eyes looked. (After all, the eyes are the window to the soul.) Did those eyes reveal something?

You can combine a lot of small things, like conversations around the kitchen table. A picture frame or piece of furniture sees a lot and might recognize certain feelings. It may see two sides, like how children act when Mom and Dad are home versus when they're gone.

If it's an object in the kitchen, it's easy to include family foods, eating habits (like always eating together), ways we eat (he's sloppy, she dainty), and favorite recipes. An object in the front room might see our manners around company. That same object might get stories we would tell the neighbors, or see the friends who pass through quickly on their way to someplace more fun and less formal. Maybe your front room is the hub of activity. What would be seen in there?

Maybe you'll get some stories of ancestors that you were never told. You can tell some of your stories that your family isn't supposed to know because you don't feel comfortable telling them, but you really want your descendants to know them.

When recording the story of an ancestor—maybe one you've heard but don't think is recorded yet—you don't really know the emotions because you weren't there, but you can often imagine what those emotions might have been. You might say, "If I had been there, I would have felt . . ." or "I think they might have felt . . ."

Think about this for a while and come up with something you can write about, or tuck the idea away until you come across a story where it works better than other ways. Maybe you'll be working on something and decide that this is a better way to write it.

Whatever you choose to do, build it into a revealing family story. Refer to "Stories by Students and Other Writings" in Part III of this book for some examples.

"Poetry and writing can be outlets to express the depth of pain, release stress, and bring peace."

—Janet

Many have used the idea of writing being an outlet. I wrote this quote, but I don't really take credit since the basic idea has been used in hundreds of different ways.

Highs, Lows, and Turning Points

You don't have to write about all the suggestions in this book. This one may be difficult, but it could be a good one if you choose to use it.

Think about the highs and lows in your life. We all have them. Look at a low time in life. Write some details. Now look at a high spot in your life, and write details about that as well.

Now record the turning points. You were going one direction (down) when something caused a change of direction. What was it? Can you remember why you turned? Was it a conscious effort, a determination to do better? Or did something outside yourself prompt you to change?

Think about why you chose those specific highs and lows. What made them stand out in your memory? Be sure to include that in your story.

Be sure your reader knows how you felt, why you were low, and how you got up again. Our descendants will need help overcoming their lows. Sharing how you did it may be just what they'll need. Also, let them know the real reason, deep down, for the high.

We are not always in a high spot. That isn't the way life is. We don't want them to expect their lives to always run smoothly or always be good. If they think our life was always good, they may expect that theirs will be unrealistically perfect. We don't want to give the opposite impression either. We want them to see that life is good but not easy.

Maybe you want to add something like this: "Because you are related to me, I know you can do hard things too. You can grow to be a better version of you as time goes on. I know I have made it through by following the Lord's direction."

Remember, don't try to be someone else—just be the best you. Heavenly Father knows what we are capable of, so let Him help. We can serve Him by serving our descendants in this way.

“Hardship, suffering, disappointment, failure, and faith, but always leading to ultimate triumph, have been the common lot of the faithful—beginning with Adam and Eve, to Noah, Abraham, Jacob, Joseph, Moses, Lehi, Joseph Smith, especially Jesus Christ, and everyone who followed after them. . . . Suffering and joy are not incompatible, but essential companions. You can suffer and never know joy, but you can’t have joy without suffering.”

—Lawrence E. Corbridge[32]

WORLD EVENTS

What things that happened in the world around you do you remember? Make a list of everything you can think of. Include events in your country, your state, and your city. You may want to use the internet to find out more and then decide if you need to add them to your list or not.

Take time to consider how these events affected your life at the time it happened. Do you still feel emotions as you think about it? Make short notes after each one that had any effect on you.

Why do we want to list these? Is it important to let our descendants know what happened in our world and how it affected us? Yes! The scriptures are filled with events that occurred during that time. Can you grasp the feelings of some of the writers about these situations? How does it help you? Remember, you are writing to help your descendants and anyone who may read your book.

Some things are important to history. You may be a witness to something that the world is now saying didn't happen. Your account can be very important.

A couple of my class groups and I came up with some world events, which I've included in the lists section in Part II of this book (see page 137), but you will be able to come up with a lot more as you review your life. Use the list if you wish to help you get started. Write about the ones that most affected you.

After you have your list of events, go back and write as much as you can recall (at least a sentence) about the ones you remember. Maybe you'll want to do a little more research to find more details, especially on ones that were important to you. Finally, pick the ones you want to write about. Save the list (with short notes) for your descendants, but add stories and details for at least a couple of events.

Be descriptive. Use plenty of adjectives (see the adjective list in the back of the book), and include emotions. How did it affect you? Do you remember noticing the effect it had on people around you? Be sure to include how you felt at the time and later.

If you have special memories connected with the event, pay attention to things like where you were and what you were doing. Do you remember what immediately followed your finding out? Did you suddenly feel insecure? Did you stare in unbelief? You should include these in stories.

How will you convey these feelings to your family? It isn't always easy to express ourselves in the way we need to for this, but you can. Write how you feel as you remember that time. Be sure to include these emotions, label them, and explain. You might relate it to something you think they would relate to. Be mindful of how people are now trying to change history, and be sure you include the truth—how it was, how you saw it, and how it affected you and others around you, even in simple ways. Don't sugarcoat anything.

If you were personally involved, or someone close to you was, you may have more you could include than you want to. It is important to remember that the Lord knows what you need to use and what you need to put away. Write everything, then ask for His help. He will help you. He cares about you, and He cares about your future posterity. He also knows what they will need and how you can help.

If you were more personally involved in something—like a war, a bombing, 9/11, or other challenging happenings that are extremely difficult to write about—you may consider using one of the other methods of writing to help you record your feelings without opening yourself up to remembered pains.

"You should never give up. No matter how hard the situation is, always believe that something beautiful is going to happen."[33]

"Remember, all good things have their price."

—Janet

There are many similar quotes out there. This idea has been quoted hundreds of times.

Sometimes It's Better with Help

We are here on earth to help each other, and sometimes we need to be willing to ask for help. Things in our lives are better with other people. Life is just that way.

Think about the stories of your life. How many of them were just about you? On the other hand, how many of your stories involved someone else? I would suppose that most of them involve two or more people.

Let's think about some stories from your life. Maybe you want to use one you already wrote. However you do it, narrow it down to a few stories. Which one of those stories would be better if it included the point of view of someone else who was there? How did *they* see it? Did they see something you missed, or maybe just had a different perspective on it? Or perhaps they were part of the story before you came in.

You are writing your personal history. You have a story that could be better or clearer by including certain details you don't know about.

So, let's try it this way:

1. Write the story, using all you can remember, or pick one you've already written.
2. Contact another person who was involved in the story. Get their side of the story. Write it out as they told it.
3. Now you have to decide what you are going to do with the new information.

Once you have the other story, you have several possibilities about what to do with it:

- You may wish to just tell the story from two different points of view. If so, the reader will now see how people see things differently.
- You may decide to write the story using your side and the other person's side blended together. You now have more details and more information but still one story.
- You may want to stick with your original story. Maybe you decided you didn't like the other point of view. That's alright too. After all, it's your life, your story, and your world. It should reflect you, not someone else.

Your choice will really depend on the story. Was the other person's part just another point of view, or did it fill in details needed to make the story more clear and complete? Either way you decide to do it is great. Just remember your reader and think about which is best for them. Make it interesting, knowledgeable, and fun, and make it *you*.

When I did this the first time, I found two stories, both involving the same person. While working on the first story, I asked the other person and got details that had happened before I became part of the story. These facts were an important part of the overall story. I blended the two sides together and got a more complete, better story. However, with the second story, when I asked about it, he just said, "Tell me more of what *you* remember." Turns out he didn't remember the situation at all and was glad to hear the story.

Who knows what you will find? Just have fun and share with your own zest.

"We are all apprentices in a craft where no one ever becomes a master."

—Ernest Hemingway[34]

He is, of course, speaking about writing. No need to get discouraged.

“No matter how bleak the chapter of our lives may look today, because of the life and sacrifice of Jesus Christ, we may hope and be assured that the ending of the book of our lives will exceed our grandest expectations.”

—President Dieter F. Uchtdorf[35]

Weather

Let's try something. Envision yourself as a child . . . and now add snow. Let your mind wander back. What experiences come to mind? Write at least a few notes to remind you.

Perhaps snow wasn't part of your life. If so, use rain or something else. Include descriptions, and don't be afraid to be a little creative. This is a good subject to help you find your creative side and let it out. Add some detail for interest that adds to the story but doesn't detract from the facts.

How would you describe a snow drift, or a very large rain puddle? How about a tornado, or just a fast-moving storm cloud? What words could you use that would bring you thoughts to life? Sometimes the best words are ones you wouldn't think to use in this spot.

Think about someone who has never seen snow or a tornado or other weather you have experienced in your life. Remember, never assume they know.

As always, how did it make you feel? Were you grateful, thrilled, frightened? Did you have to stop a minute and catch your breath? Add emotion. Explain how you were affected. Did you call on the Lord to help you? That would be an important detail. Is your story starting to come together?

There is a list of weather for you in Part II (see page 134). I included the seasons because even though they aren't really weather, they are definitely related to weather. What weather might we expect with a particular season?

Think about how weather affects your life. Do you have a favorite kind of weather? Maybe you like the sunshine, or maybe spring is your favorite time of the year. Does the cold make your bones ache? Does the heat make you dizzy? And of course there are allergies that so many of us deal with. Take a minute and consider what weather is your favorite and why.

Are there a lot of stories springing to life in your mind? Write notes as a reminder for everything you think of, whether on this subject or not. Start writing a list of things you need to include in your stories.

When you're ready, write one good story. You may find you have more, and that's great. I didn't say you can only write one story per subject. Write all you feel.

Some storms or weather patterns you might wish to discuss with family to get another view point, like how they remember a particular storm. Think in general: how does the weather affect your life?

“If life is worth living, its deeds are worth recording.”

—John Rohn[36]

"If you are on the right path, it will always be uphill."

—President Henry B. Eyring[37]

Knowledge of Your Fathers

The prophet Mormon wrote, "Know ye that ye *must* come to the knowledge of your fathers" (Mormon 7:5; emphasis added). Remember the research paper (see page 140) we have previously discussed?

Mormon is talking to us *and* to our descendants. If we don't write, how are our descendants going to be able to be obedient to the commandments to know their fathers?

Now, you may think your life isn't important and that this verse is talking about your grandfather. Not true! Your life *is* important. If you're living right, which simply means you're doing your best, you will be a great example to your family. You stand in the middle of generations gone and generations to come. It is your responsibility. As President Gordon B. Hinckley said, "Do not become a weak link in the chain of your generations."[38]

Write your history. Write it so they will want to read it.

I know I've said all this before, but we all need to be reminded. So, today I want you to go back and review what you've written about. Remember to add details and feelings and put your life into your stories so your readers will be a part of it. Like I've mentioned, never assume they know what you are talking about because they may not.

Next, go through the list of subjects in this book from the beginning and find one you haven't covered, or one where you need to do some more. Or perhaps write a story from the notes you have been making as you've gone through your days.

Finally, use what you've been learning and start to write. Are you ready to share something inspirational and uplifting?

"Having trouble while writing? Maybe you're trying too hard. Just relax and let your memory work, have faith, pray, and try again."

—Janet

ACCIDENTS

When we think about accidents, our first thought is usually about automobiles, but there are a lot of other possibilities as well.

Let's start by reviewing your life. Make a list of the accidents that you were involved in. Your list will probably need more than a couple words for each—maybe a sentence or more. Now add ones that affected your life even though you weren't personally involved in them. Finally, make another list of accidents that *didn't* happen—ones that were close, near misses, but for some reason were averted.

Accidents are a very visual thing. As you write about them, use lots of adjectives to describe what happened. Your readers need to be part of your experience.

There is always something spiritual that can come out as you describe an accident. They can be very emotional. You may not wish to tell about it in your own words. One incident that I wrote about is long, but most of consists of newspaper clippings and descriptions. Mostly my words are about the emotions, what I did, and how I handled the situation.

This subject can be very challenging to write about, especially if you were emotionally involved. Remember that there are other ways to write, like as a news article or from the point of view of an inanimate object. You can do it any way that works for you. Just know that there are some incidents in your life that should be recorded because of your personal growth from the situation. You may not have recognized that growth for many years, but it came. If you haven't seen it yet, that's understandable. Just write what is a part of you now. You can go back later and add what you have realized or what you remembered.

Remember, as you ponder accidents, think of it from two sides: ones that happened and ones that didn't. And if you look carefully, you can see the Lord's hand in both kinds. Be sure to show that.

What about the ones that didn't happen? They may be more important than ones that did, if the reason they didn't was a matter of inspired direction that you followed. Also, record ones that did happen that you could have avoided had you listened. I know I sometimes talk myself out of inspiration, and I'm sure I'm not the only one.

Start with the background. What was going on? Add the point that the accident would have or could have happened. Very carefully describe what happened. Where did the accident stop? What prevented it? Who did something that prevented the accident?

Be sure to involve your emotions. When you realized how close you came to something terrible, did you have to take some time to collect yourself? Or did that come later? Sometimes it takes a little time for things to hit us, even after it has completely passed.

Try to share enough details that the reader knows why you are sharing this story. However, be careful not to get yourself all upset with the memory. Not all of our accidents need to be told, but some could give others strength to handle some challenge that will come along.

"You can't use up creativity. The more you use, the more you have."

—Maya Angelou[39]

Do you get discouraged or wonder if your reader will misunderstand what you're trying to say? You're not the only one that has ever felt that way. Listen to how Moroni felt about the Book of Mormon:

__Ether 12:23–26__

23 And I said unto him: Lord, the Gentiles will mock at these things,
because of our weakness in writing; for Lord thou hast made us mighty in
word by faith, but thou hast not made us mighty in writing; for thou hast
made all this people that they could speak much, because of the Holy Ghost
which thou hast given them;
24 And thou hast made us that we could write but little, because of
the awkwardness of our hands. Behold, thou hast not made us mighty in
writing like unto the brother of Jared, for thou madest him that the things
which he wrote were mighty even as thou art, unto the overpowering of
man to read them.
25 Thou hast also made our words powerful and great, even that we
cannot write them; wherefore, when we write we behold our weakness, and
stumble because of the placing of our words; and I fear lest the Gentiles
shall mock at our words.
26 And when I had said this, the Lord spake unto me, saying: Fools
mock, but they shall mourn; and my grace is sufficient for the meek, that
they shall take no advantage of your weakness.

Church Callings

One thing that can have a great effect on our spiritual growth is the callings we have faithfully fulfilled in our years as members of The Church of Jesus Christ (or whatever church you may serve in). How we fulfill them, what we accomplish, and how we grow can also have an effect on our descendants. So spend a little time and figure out something you can write about on this topic.

Maybe some things you did were not official callings but still gave you some growth and added to your spiritual strength. Don't leave those out.

Let's start by making a list of each calling you've had in the Church. That will be easier, of course, if you have them written down. If not, that's okay. As you work on it, it'll come back to you.

Try going through each organization, just as a way to help remember, or maybe think about where you lived, especially if you moved around. Come up with your list of callings and then add dates as accurately as you can.

Where did you live? Be specific, naming the church unit, city, state, and so on. How long did you have the calling? If you have dates, include them. Also include how you felt about the calling, like what you feel you accomplished and what you learned from having that calling.

You may wish to include strengths you gained from this service. Do you feel like you became a better person? Did you help someone while serving?

Have you ever had a calling you felt wasn't from the Lord? If so, how did you handle it? Did you support His leader as the Lord does? Did that feeling change anything? Or did you just do your best and move on?

Have you ever said, or just thought, "The Lord's will be done"? If so, what was the situation? You could explain a time you felt that way and how it affected you.

Do you have any regrets regarding a calling? Something you wish you had done better? Maybe there's someone you later realized you could have helped, but at the time you didn't recognize a need you could have filled. Pointing out your feelings may help your reader be more observant so they won't have the same feelings.

Who did you work with? Anyone that stood out? Was someone particularly challenging to work with or especially great to work with?

Did you have any callings that no longer exist? If so, explain in more detail what the responsibility was.

Have you thought of a story yet? If so, start writing. If not, expand your list more with details and notes that might trigger a story.

As always, keep in mind, "Never assume they know what you're talking about." Even if that calling still exists now, it may not by the time someone reads your story in the future. The calling may have changed a lot in how it functions. Include details, struggles, and your growth.

Hopefully you have a story, but if not, don't worry—just move on. At the very least, leave a list with some explanations in your history. There are other ways to write, such as an article or an essay. A story might be easier using an inanimate object, like telling it from the perspective of a notebook you carried with you to meetings.

"True stories well told can inspire, caution, entertain, and instruct."[40]

"There is no exercise better for the heart than reaching down and lifting people up."

—John Holmes[41]

A Story to Lift and Encourage

A while ago, one of the speakers in my sacrament meeting said, "We tend to recall more vividly the mistakes of our past, but the gospel encourages us to not be discouraged by our low spots in life but rather to move forward with strength and determination." (And I would also add faith.)

So, how can we write so we can help our descendants do just that? We can show them the need for strengths in *their* lives through stories from *our* lives. We can help them see, "My great-grandparents handled hard things, so I can too—because they passed strengths down to me."

First, have a story in mind that you want to tell. Now envision a scene. Think about the scene you wish to create, and list everything that comes to mind as you remember it.

Next, give the facts. Include the essentials: who, what, when, where, why, and how. You may not need all of these in your story, but at least consider them all. Facts add interest and understanding.

Lastly, be sure to explain things clearly. Don't assume the reader knows anything about this scene. When it fits, bring a little romance, mystery, or fun into your stories.

Remember, the words you use are important. Be sure to include the miracles that happened during this trial or time of life.

"Your best *is* enough.
Your goals *are* important.
Your dreams *are* possible.
Your feelings *are* valid."[42]

"Always believe that something wonderful is about to happen."[43]

See the wonder in your life and write about it.

It's Your Story, and You Should Tell It

Consider this quote from Roots Tech: "There are some moments of life that I have to wonder if my three oldest children were growing up in the same house. Their impressions of the same events vary widely. Somewhere in there is the correct version, but to each of them their perception is their reality—their truth. So that's why it's important for us to tell our own story. We wouldn't want anyone else to tell our truth, our feelings, or the intimate details of our lives."[44]

That is why I have worked to create a way to make writing your stories fun and reasonably easy to record. I hope it is helping you. It's important. You don't really want someone else to try to share your feelings or the intimate details of your life. Maybe they won't see it the way you do, or they might miss facts that are important. The story can totally change by missing just a few details. Your story isn't boring, so write it with pizzazz.

Everyone deserves to be remembered, and we want to be remembered for our best selves. Some people only see what's wrong. Others only see the shiny side, missing the trials that made them shine. We shouldn't be remembered at our worst or seen as perfect; neither is accurate. Only *you* really know who you are.

At this point, you have thought about the wonders in your life. You have taken notes of the things you are grateful for. You have gotten in touch with the inner you through food and fun. You have been reminded that you are worth more than you have accepted. You have seen the fun and some trials. So the question is, are you ready? I think you are.

Today, we are going to reach for a challenge. We are going to write "Who I Am."

I Am—Not I Did

Let's say you were going to be the speaker at a conference of some sort. The person who introduces you would probably point out some of your accomplishments that qualify you to give that particular speech, but is that who you really are?

What if you introduce yourself starting with "I am" and then explain who you *are* rather than what you have *done*? Or, even better, what if someone who really knows you introduced you this way?

You might say something like, "I'm a wife, mother, grandmother, and great-grandmother. I am the daughter of good parents who taught me to work hard. They taught me to love nature, the natural beauty of our world. They taught me to love the Lord. I am blessed with *so* very much in the nonmaterial sense. The Lord has blessed me with talents and the opportunity to use them to better my life and help others too. Most of all, I am a child of God who loves me and wants me to return to Him one day. I look forward to that day, but in between now and then . . ." This paragraph is good, but it still only touches the surface of who you *are*.

Consider what your Heavenly Father thinks of you. Trust me, He sees a whole lot more in you than you see in yourself, and especially more than you are willing to admit. We all have a fear of pride. When you're writing your history, especially this one, let it all out. Consider reading your patriarchal blessing for some help.

Write something about who you are. Think about prophets through the years—prophets in the Old Testament, New Testament, Book of Mormon, and this dispensation. Think about your ancestors; what would you want to know about who *they* are? This one could take a long time, but it's important. If you get started and don't know where to continue, pray about it and maybe put it on the shelf for a while. But sooner or later, get it done.

This might be a good opening when you put your history story book together. Think about who you really are. Your personality should pop up here, not what you've done. What you've done should creep into your other stories.

Remember that you're suppose to be honest, not humble. Include your talents, your strengths, your God-given abilities, and your heavenly gifts.

Include your loves, your dislikes, and some of your weaknesses (but don't get carried away). Share some opportunities you have had to use these talents and strengths to help others. Show your faith, vision, and testimony. Try to see yourself as the Lord sees you. Then write it.

You don't need to share this with anyone in this life besides yourself. Leave it for after you're gone if you wish, unless it would help to have input from others. Maybe you could discuss this one with others so they can help you. For example, does someone else know your strengths better than you do? Perhaps visit with them.

I wrote a lot of mine by quoting what other people have said about me. I included a few things that are "just part of who I am," like my smile, my tendency to walk in bare feet, and so on. You have things that are just part of who you are. Be sure they are in your introduction.

You may wish to do this a different way. We have talked about writing in different ways, and one of those may work well for this topic. Consider using an inanimate object's point of view, or write an article as if you're writing about a famous person. In Part III of this book, you will find another idea by one of my students that she was willing to share (see "I Am" on pages 153 and 154). Whichever way you decide to do it, make sure it is accurate. You can't be modest with this one. Tell it like it is.

Have you ever wondered, as I have, who you really are? Well, this is a chance to do a little discovering, or a little confessing you may say. Dig deep. This one is mostly for you. It is important that you accept your strengths. The Lord has blessed you so you can bless others. Accept that. You won't help others if you don't accept yourself and the God-given strengths you have been blessed with.

“Include the Lord in your writings. He wants you to write for you and for your descendants. He knows what they will need.”

—Janet

Nephi tells us why he kept a record and therefore why we should do so as well.

"I, Nephi, having been born of goodly parents, therefore I was taught somewhat in all the learning of my father; and having seen many afflictions in the course of my days, nevertheless, having been highly favored of the Lord in all my days; yea, having had a great knowledge of the goodness and the mysteries of God, therefore I make a record of my proceedings in my days" (1 Nephi 1:1).

Why?

- Because I had good parents.
- Because I was taught and educated.
- Because I had afflictions in life.
- Because I was highly favored of the Lord.
- Because I had great knowledge of the goodness of God.
- Therefore, I make a record of my days.

Now really, aren't these things (at least a few of them) reasons for you to write as well? And you probably have even more good reasons.

EDUCATION

We spend many years getting an education, Some continue longer. You probably had teachers you loved and some you didn't. You likely had problems along the way, for example being shy, insecure, teased, or otherwise maltreated. But you probably had plenty of successes as well, like being a class officer or a top student.

Did you go to preschool? What about kindergarten? Maybe you went only to twelve grades.

So, start thinking. What were some highlights, like classes you loved, subjects that came easy, or a class you really learned a lot in? What about the opposite—classes that you disliked, were difficult, or you felt were a waste of time?

How many different schools did you attend? You may want to describe the building, especially if you had some kind of attachment to it. Was there a particular place you liked to play? Did you have a favorite seat? What about the lunch room? If you like architecture, you might relate to the style. You could research the building if it was one of those old majestic structures. Do you have pictures?

How can we approach sharing our education with our families? Perhaps you can consider how your school days were different from your children or grandchildren's school days. How was your education different from that of your grandparents or other family members?

You may need to make a list of what is important to you and just include a few details about each. Hopefully, a story has begun to shine through. Was there a tragedy during your school years? Did something wonderful happen?

Put together a story from your perspective. If you dig deep within yourself, you may be surprised what is there. If you don't have a story right now, just make your list with as many details as you can think of and put it away for a later time.

The world is constantly changing, so use details—put it all in.

Remember two things I say often: "Never assume they know what you're talking about," and "Always weave your testimony through your stories. Always pay attention to the spiritual components in your life stories."

"All life is an experiment. The more experiments you make the better."

—Ralph Waldo Emerson[45]

"To make a difference
in someone's life,
you don't have to
be brilliant, rich,
beautiful, or perfect.
You just have
to care."

—Mandy Hale[46]

Challenging Times

You may wish to call it a trial or not, but the truth is that each one of us experiences challenging times during our lives.

Our experiences matter. Not just because of how you feel at the time, but because they leave lasting traces in your brain that affect your life. If you write about the good in your experiences, you reinforce the positive in your brain. Your attention is like a spotlight that vacuums up whatever you focus on. It highlights what it lands on, then sucks it into your brain for better or for worse. So, as you write, try to be positive. That does not mean you should leave out everything that wasn't perfect or even positive—your descendants need to know your life wasn't perfect. However, they also need to know that you found it good even when it was problematic, even if finding the good took you a while.

Weave your faith into your stories the same way it has been woven into your life. Weave it in such a way that, as they read, their minds will be focused on faith, strength, and growth. They will see the good in life that comes in spite of trials. They should be able to see the humor in life and gain strength, giving them what they need to meet their challenges.

Write about a difficult time in your life. Remember to include the pain, the hardship, and maybe even the occasional depression, but also include your faith. You made it through the tough times, and they can too. Remember that what they focus on affects their brains also. Share both sides of the story with them. Recall the struggle, the prayers, the miracles, the inspiration that came to help you through, and especially what you learned. Take a lot of time. Let your feelings come through. Include emotions. Talk to your loved ones to get another perspective if they were involved enough to know details about it. Did your positive attitude shine through, or did you have to find it later?

Remember, *always* include the Lord in your writing. He knows what your descendants need. He can help you know what to write about and what details should be included.

Emotions are a big part of trials, so be sure to include them. Don't leave out all the times of depression or even anger. Did you talk to yourself a lot about not letting this get you down? How did you hang on? Did you feel alone, or did you have plenty of support from family or friends? Point out that the Lord was always there, as long as you would accept Him. Let your spiritual strength come out. Don't hide it. Don't try to be too humble. You can always use the scriptures as a guide. There you'll find many examples of trials and the strengths that people used to deal with those hard times.

So, first decide which trial or hard time you want to start writing about. Then get to work!

"When your story has sat for a while (cold) and you're ready to check it, read it aloud. When possible, read to someone else. Children are great—you get a bright perspective from them.

Pay attention to questions they ask. Then decide if you need to add something or leave something out.

Even if you just read to yourself, reading aloud will help you discover what you like and don't like."

—Janet

Jobs

Have you ever had a job that was unusual? Maybe something that added excitement to life or provided an engaging challenge? Was there ever something strange that happened at work? Did you work with someone noteworthy, fascinating, or otherwise interesting?

Whether you thought your job was exciting or boring, it was what you did to be self-sufficient, and that's important. At first, you may think this is something you don't want to write about, but as you get going, you should be able to see the interest.

Let's make list of all the jobs you have had. Give yourself time. Add details about the skills needed to get the job and what you learned from it. It might help to find an old resume.

Did you mow lawns or deliver papers or tend the neighbor's children? Start there since that's where you started. Continue until you have a complete list, at least as complete as your memory comes up with for now. Whatever you have done, it had an influence on your life, and hopefully for good. We learn something from everything and everyone in our lives, so it needs to be recorded in our personal history.

Pick one job, maybe your favorite. Write down everything you think of when you think about that job. Allow your memory to float back to the time you worked there. You should be able to come up with at least a good sentence about everything you've done.

Add how you obtained the job, what you did there, people you worked with or interacted with, dates started and ended, where it was, and maybe why you wanted that job. How did you accomplish what was needed? Include all that applies to you and the job.

Was there a job you didn't get, or you turned down, that was important to you? Maybe that's something that needs to be included in your history. Explain its importance and why you didn't get the job. For example, I turned down a job after it was offered to me because they expected me to work on Sundays and I wasn't willing to do so. That one I will include because I really wanted the job.

If you want, you can include jobs that we don't typically call jobs, like mother, father, housewife, gardener, mechanic, or handyman—some of the things you did that gave you life experience but didn't really improve your finances. Actually, these things *do* improve your finances. The things you produce (or the services you provide) may not count as income, but they do reduce expenses and therefore improve your financial situation. They are also part of who you are, part of being self-reliant, and part of building you.

Use these experiences as examples of your personal growth. Include descriptions, details, feelings, and attitudes. Your readers may not know what you're talking about if you lightly mention something that is part of your life because it may not be part of their lives. Think of your ancestors. What would you like to know more about? Consider your job. What was it really like, and how did you do it? What kinds of things did you do as a housewife? What do you do, or have you done, that makes you a better spouse? Explain the appliances, office equipment, and vehicles you used, the tasks you did, and whatever else was involved. You can be very descriptive here, just as with other subjects.

Perhaps there really isn't a story on this subject. That's alright, but at least include some information about what you've done. You may just wish to include the list in your history as jobs you've had, with a little bit of information about each one. If you have a story that goes with a certain job, write it. If not, maybe include a description of a typical work day, written like a story. Use what's right for you.

Whatever you do, remember that you are writing for two reasons: (1) for you, to help you know you're a good person and have done good in your life, and (2) for your descendants to help them get through their tough times. So be sure you allow your strengths, your testimony, and your love for life and for your Savior to creep into your stories.

“When you survived cancer, or something else, you were given a second chance. How are you going to use it? Your life is valuable! Share it.”

—Janet

“The worst thing
you write is
better than
the best thing
you did not
write.”

—Janet

Spiritual Topics

When writing, remember to include your feelings, thoughts, attitudes, and interesting facts. These are especially important elements when talking about spiritual things. They are also especially difficult. Keep trying. Find something you want to share, then relax, pray, and write. Don't try to force your memory—just put the idea in your thoughts, and when something comes, write.

Put yourself back in time. How did you feel? Were there tears? Other signs of emotion? Was this experience personal or a shared time?

You may need to consult your journal for some help. Be specific, and remember to add details

How do you feel about your religion, in general and specifically? How important is it to you?

If you have a conversion story, be sure to tell it in as great of detail as you possibly can. If you grew up in the Church, your conversion may have been a gradual process. Still think about how and when you felt the stirrings of testimony. There must be something you would want to share with those you love.

Did you have an experience when you knew the Book of Mormon was true? Or when you grasped the amazingness of the Savior's love for you? Or a time when the incredible power of the Atonement of Jesus Christ just really struck you? Pull out the moments that have built your spiritual strength.

Add your thoughts and feelings about prophets in general, and then about the specific ones who have touched your life. How have you felt about the prophets you've known, even from afar? Did you ever meet a prophet? If so, be sure to include that story. Help your readers feel the spiritual strength of the situation—your spiritual growth.

Here are a few more areas of your spiritual life to consider recording:

- *Spiritual education*: formal (seminary, institute, special classes, firesides) and informal (learning on your own, personal study, prayer, quiet moments)
- *Family and friends*: family home evenings, special times together with family and friends, learning from parents as a child, learning from others through life (teachers, friends, classes)
- *Missionary work*: callings (full-time, stake, ward), missionary experiences, following the prophet's direction
- *Volunteer work*: being a guide for a Church site, other experiences

- When you helped make someone's life better or were the answer to someone's prayer

Just one last thought about this topic: if you ponder about your conversion, you will discover things you didn't realize. I've only lately been thinking about my conversion. I have always felt like I came that way—with a testimony. And I think I did, but there is still a conversion process that takes a whole lifetime. I need to consider the progress I've made so far. Perhaps you do too.

Spiritual Experiences

Writing about some of our spiritual experiences is very challenging. Some are personal and should not be shared with too many. We share only as the Spirit directs us, so how do we decide what to write?

I suggest writing them all. You do *not* need to share them while you are here, but someday it will be important that someone knows those stories. So you write them. Share the ones you feel to share now, and tuck the rest away for after you have moved on to another life. Mark them and indicate where they are so your reader will know they are valuable.

Remember to include the following:

- *Your feelings*: How did you feel at the time and later as you think about it?
- *Your thoughts*: What thoughts went through your mind during the experience and now as you reflect on it? Can you feel how your mind was maybe racing and not focusing? What were you really thinking?
- *Your attitudes*: Did this happen because of a certain attitude or inspiration that led you to something? Think about your frame of mind.
- *Interesting facts*: Include every detail that has anything to do with the story or situation.

These things are always important, but when sharing your spiritual experiences, they are absolutely vital, even though it can be especially difficult to express. Just keep trying.

Here are a few areas for you to consider as you work to remember your spiritual experiences. Think about God's hand in your life in these and other ways.

Miracles

Consider any miracles you've experienced. There may be a need for some background before the story can be understood by your reader, like what led up to the situation. "Never assume they know what you are talking about."

What happened? Include anything you should share. Be prayerful and selective.

Some things are personal and ought to be tucked away for later. Listen to the promptings of the Spirit. If you feel it is just for you, you may wish to record it and tuck it away where it won't be found until after you are gone. Or you may wish to not record it until later. But just a warning—our memories tend to fade as we age.

President Eyring said we need to record the miracles in our lives.[47] It helps us to learn to recognize them.

Blessings

Recording your blessings is another great idea. Gratitude may bring things to your mind that you could share about. You may wish to just leave a list of what you are grateful for and explain some things. You do it your way.

Have you become grateful for something later that you were hardly aware of at the time? If so, you may want to explain more. For example, I have sometimes later recognized that something I thought was a problem was actually preventing something worse. There are blessings in our lives daily, so there really should be something every day that you can record.

Prayers and Answers

When it comes to answered prayers, some background is definitely needed. For instance, how long did you pray for that specific thing? Has this been a lifelong prayer, or did the answer come quickly?

When, where, and how did the answer come? Was is all at once, or was it something that came a little at a time over a period of time?

Revelation

Revelation or inspiration comes in many different ways. It may be as feelings, or just a thought that comes that you don't initially recognize as heavenly guidance. Also, visions really do still happen. You could have a dream (or a daydream) where you didn't know if you were awake or asleep. Visions sometimes come almost like you are remembering something that you had forgotten. Occasionally, when the message is urgent, revelation can even come as a direct voice, like someone speaking to you. There may also be times when the Spirit puts words in your mouth, like when you say something insightful without it really passing through your mind first.

So, record what the inspiration was and how it came. Use as much explanation as you can. Use your senses, or whatever adjectives needed, to explain. Help the reader to feel the Spirit of the experience. If you feel it again as you're writing, it will help.

Have you ever realized, at some later time, that you had received a revelation? Was it intended just for you? Maybe after the task was completed, you recognized where the direction came from.

And, of course, there's the big question: what did you do about it? If it was direction for something you needed to accomplish, somewhere you needed to go, or someone you needed to call or help, did you follow through? Recording this part of the story tells your descendants a lot about you and will help them learn to follow through on their own revelations.

Testimony

You should record, more than once in your life, your testimony. Include how important it is you. Explain some things about your testimony, like how you obtained it and how it was strengthened over the years. You might make note of stories you have previously written that have to do with your testimony. If you mention stories, be sure to put a footnote stating where they can be found. (Or if they're in the same book you compiled, include the title and page.)

If you are a Christian, your testimony should include your belief in and how you feel about Jesus Christ—as your Savior, as the Son of God, and as an example to you.

If you are a member of The Church of Jesus Christ of Latter-day Saints, your testimony should also include how you feel about the following:

- Joseph Smith (as a prophet and as a man)
- The Book of Mormon (the truth of it, your feelings about it)
- Other prophets today and throughout history

Is there a prophet you particularly loved? One that specifically strengthened you? We all have certain people who are "on our wavelength"—people we learn from more than others. Include ones from the scriptures who have helped you.

Your testimony could include other things about your spiritual side that you believe or know to be true. Share whatever you feel—your love, your strength, where your guidance comes from, why you are who you are.

In conclusion, write all your stories you can find for this section. Some of them you will include in your life story to give your family now or soon. The rest you will put away somewhere safe where they will be found when you're gone. Mark which ones you want your posterity to read, and mark which ones you want to end up in the trash. I have a file specifically marked to be destroyed. You figure out what's right for you and your descendants.

Whatever you do, do *not* hide what you know! Others can't grow from your God-given gifts, talents, and strengths if you don't share them. They were meant to be used to lift others. Don't be shy and don't shrink—just share and let it all out. Who are you? Let your descendants see the person the Lord sees in you.

Writing about spiritual experiences is possibly the most important thing you should write. Some moments you may not have recognized as spiritual experiences, but when you take time to contemplate God's hand in your life, you may be more likely to see the blessings or even miracles that were there the whole time.

"Dear love of
my life, I just
want you to
know how much
I've enjoyed
annoying you
all this time,
and how excited
I am to keep
doing so for
all eternity."[48]

A Great Love Story

I was recently thinking about Joseph Smith and Emma. I would call that a great love story. With all that they went through, they worked things out together. They were there for each other through unbelievable trials.

What about Adam and Eve? That has to be a great love story.

What about you and your spouse? Is there a great love story there? How are you going to portray that love, the strength you built over the years, to your future generations? Do you think it's important that they know you too have a great love story? I do.

That love story is something that was built over years of time and effort. It wasn't always easy. It wasn't always happy. You persevered through years of ups and downs until, in the end, it became a great love story.

Now, I know not all of you have reached that point yet. Some of us are at the stage where our eternal companion has moved on to another stage of life, one without pain and the weaknesses of the physical body. However, the love we shared didn't leave with them. In fact, from my perspective, I would say the love has grown and strengthened with the temporary separation and the trial of being alone.

As you write, you can think about your grandparents. What would you want to learn that would help young couples now, especially your descendants, make a growing marriage into a great love story?

I asked one of my classes, and here are some of their answers:

- I'm a girl, so I like all the mushy details. I want to know how they met and how their relationship became a marriage.
- I want to know the things we've been writing about our lives—their ups and downs, how they made it through, and how they went from falling in love to experiencing a deep love.
- Did they pray together? Specifically, how did they work out their differences and make decisions?

Part II

Lists, Lists, Lists

These are great resources to get you started if you want to use them.

Basic List

Accidents	Happened or saved from
Ancestors	Compare daily differences in life
Ancestors	Write specific information about them, what impressed you about them, what you learned from them
Animals	Pets, yours or friends', any you enjoyed
Any picture	What this picture means to you, why it's important
Be amazed	See the wonder in the world around you
Blessings	Gratitude, things you recognize and appreciate
Can't do alone	Goes with trials but can be another point of view
Church callings	Where, what, when, how you felt about it (before and after)
Clothes	Worn at different stages of life
Compare photos	Photo when young, current, what changed in between
Driver's license	Age, where, memories, how you learned to drive
Earliest memories	Whatever comes to mind when you think of childhood
Education/ schools	Where, what you learned and liked/disliked, teachers, highlights
Everyday life and things	Different than years ago, different than the future
Family activities	Family home evenings, special traditions, times together

Family reunions	How your family did them, different family groups
Favorite things	Stuff, things that bring memories
Favorites, other	Music, stories, thoughts, sayings, quotes, scriptures
Food memories	Favorite recipes, family activities, smells remembered
Fun	What you did as a child, single person, now
Games/activities	Enjoyed as a child, later, still enjoy
I am	Not I *did* but who you really *are*, don't be modest
Jobs and volunteering	What you did, people, how you obtained job, stories about it
Maps	Include maps of important places
Medical	Doctors (good and bad), health info helpful to descendants, diseases, other struggles
Memories	What you think about when your mind wanders, what's interesting
Miracles	Background and what happened, carefully selected
Neighbors and friends	Interaction with, friends developed
Occasions	Holidays, birthdays, anniversaries, celebrations
Outdoor activities	Camping, hunting, guns, tents, outdoor toys
Parades, other	Have enjoyed, significance, participated in
People	About them and how they influenced your life
Places	Lived in, otherwise part of life, cost, rent/buy
Places	Have been, visited, travel, vacations

Prayers and answers	Background, how long you prayed, when and where answer came
Prices	Cost of things at different times in life
Promises	Made, then kept or not kept, how it affected you
Religion	How important to you, testimony, story of your conversion
Religious education	Where, what your learned or liked
Revelation and inspiration	What and how, what you did about it
Scripture stories	Think of many favorites, then write stories that come to mind
Senses	Sounds, smells, sights, textures, tastes, memories
Technology	How you've seen it change
Testimony	How important, how you obtained it, related stories
Transportation	What you owned, drove, enjoyed
Trials	We all have them, note particular ones for you
Volunteering	What you did, official volunteer or just because
Where were you when . . .	Note things in history, even in your backyard
Weather	Memories triggered: water, snow, rain, etc.
Work and play	Not connected with job
World around you	Memories triggered: trees, mountains, water, etc.
World events	Significant going ons, where you were, how you felt, how it affected your life

Changes in the Last Hundred Years

Kitchen

- Sink with running water
- Cabinets
- Stove
- Refrigerator
- Microwave
- Crock pot
- Electric mixer
- Pressure cooker
- Electric pressure cooker
- Wheat grinder
- Dishwasher
- Pans, easy to clean and lightweight

Power Transportation

- Tractors
- Cars
- Trucks

Living, Dining, and Family Rooms

- Television
- Computer
- Vacuum
- Floor coverings
- Carpet
- Luxury tile
- Even wood instead of dirt

Bedrooms

- Spring mattress
- Chest of drawers
- Dresser with mirror

Bathroom

- Running water
- Shower and/or tub
- Indoor flush toilet
- Toiletries, toilet paper, soap

Miscellaneous

- Washing Machine
- Dryer
- Furnace

Office (Home or Work)

- Computer
- Calculator
- Fax machine
- Adding machine
- Telephone systems
- Telegraph
- Nice desk and chair

A Few Others from Class

- Grocery store
- Hot water
- Lights
- Electricity
- Decorative lighting
- Velcro
- Pillows
- Personal care items
- Cushioned furniture
- Cell phones
- Even the size of homes

Weather

Rain
(puddles)

Snow

Hail

Sleet

Floods

Sunshine

Wind

Strange weather
(earthquakes, tornados, hurricanes, monsoons, tsunami)

Thunder

Lightning

Sand

Sandstorm

Dust

Dismal days

Clouds
(peaceful, fast-moving)

Fog

Spring

Summer

Fall

Winter

What Has Changed in Your Life?

Some of the things you might put on your list:

- Learned to walk and talk.
- Learned to eat and feed yourself.
- Learned to dress yourself.
- Learned letters, then to read and write.
- Learned numbers, then math.
- Learned to get along with people.
- Learned to obey your parents (or not).
- Learned about your body and how it works.
- Learned to take care of your possessions.
- Learned how to keep your surrounding clean and orderly.
- Learned to ride a tricycle and then a bike.
- Learned to use a skateboard or other fun toys.
- Learned to ride a horse and later saddle it yourself.
- Learned to milk a cow.
- Learned to mow a lawn and help with a garden.
- Learned to cook and clean up after yourself.
- Learned to fix a car or who to ask for help.
- Learned to sew, to make and mend your own clothes.
- You found someone special and fell in love.
- Hopefully you learned to love the Lord and your fellow man.

The World around You

Water
- Lakes, rivers, streams

Trees
- Climbing
- Growing fruit and nuts
- Just enjoy seeing

Plants and Flowers

Mountains
- Time spent there
- Favorite spots
- Snow-capped
- Vibrant fall colors

Fires
- Backyard
- Forest
- Man-made
- Lightning

Senses
- Hear (sounds)
- Smells
- See (sights)
- Touch
- Taste

Day Sky
- Sun
- Clouds

Night Sky
- Sunrise
- Sunset
- Moon
- Stars and planets

Ground
- Grass
- Mud

Farms and Gardens

World Events

Events that happened during your life, especially ones you remember or that had an effect on your life.

- Kennedy assassinated (1963)
- First man on the moon (1969)
- Revelation for all worthy men to receive the priesthood (1978, record special memories, like first man to receive, did you know someone?)
- Floods in Salt Lake City and Davis County (1983)
- Challenger explosion (1986)
- Berlin wall came down (Nov. 9, 1989)
- The Soviet Union broke up (Dec. 25, 1991)
- Internet came into existence (1992)
- Beginning of cell phones (1990s)
- Tornado in Salt Lake City (1999)
- Conference Center built (2000)
- 9/11 (2001)
- Olympics in Utah (2002)
- Legacy Highway built (2008)
- US presidential changes
- Temples that are important to you (Bountiful Temple in Nov. 1994, Brigham City Temple in Aug. 2012)
- Temple construction throughout the world
- Stake farms
- A prophet's death (or other connection with prophets)
- Death of someone important in your area
- Wars started and/or ended (soldiers you've known, how it affected your life)
- Takeover of countries (people displaced)
- Fires in California and other areas
- Poverty
- Droughts
- Violence (bombings, school shootings)

Adjectives

abundant
advantageous
affectionate
annoying
antic
appealing
aromatic
artificial
auspicious
balanced
benevolent
brilliant
brittle
clear
clever
clownish
combustible
comely
contemplative
contemptuous
corrosive
cranky
deadly
deceptive
delicate
detestable
devastating
devoted
disastrous
discerning
discreet
envious
fashionable
fastidious
flagrant
flattering
foreboding
frugal
frustrating
generous
genuine
harsh
healthy
heavy
historic
impish
impudent
indecisive
inflammatory
inventive
irresponsible
irritating
judgemental
juicy
laughable
lavish
luminous
magnificent
malicious
menacing
meticulous
naive
nervous
obnoxious
obstinate
obtuse
old-fashioned
persistent
pervasive
petulant
prolific
pungent
radiant
rebellious
resistant
resourceful
sarcastic
seductive
self-confident
serene
serpentine
shabby
sharp
social
spasmodic
special
speedy
spirited
spontaneous
strict
subtle
superficial
suspensive
tearful
tenacious
tense
theatrical
timid
transparent
treacherous
tricky
turbulent
uncompromising
unconscious
unpleasant
unyielding
verdant
voracious
vulnerable
wicked
widespread
windy
wise
withering
zealous
zesty

PART III

STORIES BY STUDENTS AND OTHER WRITINGS

(All the stories are used with the permission of the authors.)

Research Study: "The Stories That Bind Us"

"In all of us there is a hunger, marrow-deep, to know our heritage, to know who we are and where we came from. Without this enriching knowledge, there is a hollow and yearning. No matter what our attainments in life, there is still a vacuum, an emptiness, and the most disquieting loneliness." —Alex Haley[49]

Are you going to let your descendants be lonely without ever knowing why? Think of them. We know the world today, and we also know it will only get worse. When you leave this life and get to the celestial kingdom, will you want your family to join you there in time? You can help them by simply recording stories.

There is evidence beyond the importance of stories. Want something more up-to-date, a little more modern? I came across a research study on this topic, published in *The New York Times*, and I thought it was important information for people who are writing their personal histories.

So today we take a little different approach. Because remember—one day, *you* will be someone's ancestor (if you're not already one).

Here is an excerpt of the article, written by Bruce Feiler:

> The single most important thing you can do for your family may be the simplest of all: develop a strong family narrative.
>
> I first heard this idea from Marshall Duke, a colorful psychologist at Emory University. In the mid-1990s, Dr. Duke was asked to help explore myth and ritual in American families.
>
> "There was a lot of research at the time into the dissipation of the family," he told me at his home in suburban Atlanta. "But we were more interested in what families could do to counteract those forces."
>
> Around that time, Dr. Duke's wife, Sara, a psychologist who works with children with learning disabilities, noticed something about her students.
>
> "The ones who know a lot about their families tend to do better when they face challenges," she said.
>
> Her husband was intrigued, and along with a colleague, Robyn Fivush, set out to test her hypothesis. They developed a measure called the "Do You Know?" scale that asked children to answer 20 questions.
>
> Examples included: Do you know where your grandparents grew up? Do you know where your mom and dad went to high school? Do you

> know where your parents met? Do you know an illness or something really terrible that happened in your family? Do you know the story of your birth?
>
> Dr. Duke and Dr. Fivush asked those questions of four dozen families in the summer of 2001, and taped several of their dinner table conversations. They then compared the children's results to a battery of psychological tests the children had taken, and reached an overwhelming conclusion. The more children knew about their family's history, the stronger their sense of control over their lives, the higher their self-esteem and the more successfully they believed their families functioned. The "Do You Know?" scale turned out to be the best single predictor of children's emotional health and happiness.
>
> "We were blown away," Dr. Duke said. . . .
>
> Why does knowing where your grandmother went to school help a child overcome something as minor as a skinned knee or as major as a terrorist attack?
>
> "The answers have to do with a child's sense of being part of a larger family," Dr. Duke said.[50]

I extracted only a small part of the research. The whole report is much longer, but suffice it to say that it's true. We should be able to figure that out by observation. We simply are better if we have a strong sense of belonging. History and the current world demonstrate the innate need for family to help us become our best selves.

The Tree

By Chyree Stokes

The tree was a giant oak tree, strong and sturdy, standing in the yard at my grandmother's home in Kanarraville, Utah. A stream of cool mountain water ran next to the tree, feeding and nourishing it year-round. And grass grew on either side of the little stream, beckoning everyone who passed by to sit a spell and enjoy the shade of the branches of the tree. Those branches were forever reaching out and upward, trying to take as much space as possible and continually reaching for the blue sky overhead.

This tree was enchanting and magical as it could always lure me and Jim, my brother and best friend, into its fold of branches and leaves. It was the best of the best of playground equipment two kids could ever want. A hide-out from the cornfield and corn needing to be picked, or tomatoes patches needing to be stripped, or squash needing to be gathered and wrapped in old newspaper and put away for winter.

But it was more! Its branches became beautiful horses that could be ridden for hours, and when bounced hard enough, they became bucking broncs or even big, ferocious bulls in a rodeo.

Oftentimes, the big branches became airplanes off to war and we were the pilots, strong and brave, shooting down the enemy as we snuck up on them from behind.

We became space cowboys in our rocket ship as we climbed from limb to limb to the tippy top of the giant oak. We claimed for ourselves all we could see, planets and stars of all shapes and colors and a few aliens as well.

Oh yes, what fun for two best friends who had wonderful imaginations. But you could never have convinced us it wasn't magic!

Tougher than a Bullet

Rosalee Thain
April 2022

The following story was written as an assignment to write about how some tragic event has affected the author's life.

"Once upon a time . . ." That's how fairy tales begin. And we hope they end with "happily ever after." But what happens in between is what makes us who we are.

Once there was a beautiful, caring, trusting young lady. She had a loving family, animals she loved and cared for, and friends. Life was good. Little did she know that she would soon have to be so strong, for there would be many dragons to slay.

It was a cold day, February 16, 2017. School was out and Deserae was hanging around with a couple friends. How could she have known that those "friends" were in disguise? They were not true friends and had evil on their minds.

What would make someone wonder what it would be like to kill someone? Wonder enough that they would actually shoot this loving fourteen-year-old girl in the head and leave her in a snowy canal to die alone? What would make them keep the shell casing as a trophy?

It's been five years since that night, when two mothers, their own children safe in bed, went to help search and found her barely clinging to life. Her father was there within minutes, followed by police, paramedics, family . . . a whirlwind of people helping. There were fundraisers and benefits all over the county, raising money to help with the family expenses. Our stake had a special fast for her and her family. Communities pulled together to do whatever was needed. Everyone just wanted to do something to help.

We prayed and waited anxiously for the updates on her condition.
Finally, she was awake.
She was going to make it.

After more than two months, she was released from Primary Children's Hospital, telling us all that she was tougher than a bullet. It was such a relief. But her journey was just beginning.

She had traumatic brain injury. There were bullet fragments in her brain. She was paralyzed on the left side of her body and was in constant pain.

So began the long road ahead. There would be dozens of surgeries, physical therapy, relearning skills. Eventually, she got back to school, though not full-time. She became homecoming queen and through hard work was able to graduate with her class. Instead of competing with her horse, she now spends time with her service dog, Snoopy, who knows her so well. She uses robotics to help her use her arm.

Life is not easy for Des, but you won't hear her complain. Sure, she has hard days. Days when she would just like to quit. But she doesn't. A year ago, she achieved her goal of becoming a missionary, serving as a service mission. With the help of her family, she also grows thousands of flowers to give away, which is part of how she is giving back to the community who loves her so much.

That's only the beginning of the story. There will be more dragons to slay, but she has taught me that I can also slay the dragons that stand in my way.

I look to Deserae as an example that I too can fight the good fight. That I can become stronger. That I can live happily ever after. And when needed, I can be tougher than a bullet.

These are my impressions only and are not official statements from Deserae.

Reminder from Home

Written by Donna Teeples
June 13, 2019

Doing the Moab River Run, as one of the leaders with the youth of our ward, was fun and memorable. But the real lesson came for me on the first evening of our trip.

I shared a small pup tent with one of our daughters and her two friends. After a fun and tiring day, we crawled into our sleeping bags for the evening. The girls were tired and settled down quickly, but I was restless. The night was warm, and with so many of us in the little tent, it was crowded and stuffy. I felt I needed air. I slipped out of the tent with my sleeping bag to sleep outside.

There was a concrete table and benches next to our tent, and I figured the table was a perfect platform for a bed above any little critters that might find their way into my bag! I settled down and was lying on my back looking into the heavens. I marveled at the immensity of the expanse before me. I was in awe of its beauty. I felt insignificant in this huge universe, a mere speck on this earth. I wondered how our Father in Heaven could possibly care individually about each of His children when they are as numerous as the stars in the heavens. I questioned my worth as a tiny speck in our Father's plan.

As I pondered this thought, dark clouds moved across the sky, and it looked like a storm was approaching. The clouds grew darker and I was fascinated by their growing animation as they obscured the bright moon off and on. The boiling of the clouds intensified and I was actually alarmed as I watched the storm accelerate so quickly. I felt vulnerable to the elements. The thought came to me that I might be struck by lightning, but I was so mesmerized by the scene that I was powerless to move. It was terrifying to watch, but I could not turn away. I expected a deluge at any moment.

Just when I expected the heavens to burst, I felt a drop of rain on my cheek. One drop! That was it—the storm was over! All that bluster to produce one drop of rain? But the second I felt the drop on my cheek, an amazing, wonderful feeling came over me. It was as if I were one with the universe. I no longer felt inferior but felt empowered by the thought that I was not an insignificant speck but a co-element with God's creations. It was a profound revelation. The lesson seemed prepared just for me to answer my question of personal worth and significance in His sight.

I gave thanks to my Heavenly Father for providing that lesson through a tiny raindrop. I fell into a peaceful, deep sleep.

I am reminded of this experience when we sing "How Great Thou Art."[51] I have seen the stars and heard the rolling thunder. I have felt the power He displays in the universe and in my life, and my soul sings.

Gramps and Grammy

By Shaylee Ray

We called them Gramps and Grammy, and they were my great-grandparents on my mother's side: Ira Dean Deveraux and Wilma Frederick. I remember the brick house, the long driveway on the left side, the stairs on the same side that led up to the door. I remember the creaking sound of the storm door when we opened it, and the smell of Grammy's house coming out when we opened the door to enter.

Right off to the left was the den; right in front of you was the door that led down the creaking, plastic steps to the basement; and the left led into the kitchen area with brown cupboards and bright yellow countertops. Continuing into the kitchen, there was a dining table on the left wall that always reminded me of a diner booth, and in the front, inside of the big bay window, was the dining table. Gramps had a chair in between the booth and the dining table because he would love to sit and watch the activity happening throughout the busy kitchen. I remember the drawer in the kitchen that was always stocked with Oreos, Chips Ahoy chocolate chip cookies, and other crème-centered cookies, ready for the grandkids to help themselves to, and we did!

The main living room was behind the kitchen, and there was an old desk that would hold their mail and other papers, a big counter full of pictures of all of the family members, and a rocking couch that was very popular with the kids. The couches were yellow with big, bright flower print, and the carpet was a happy green. The curtains that hung from every window were thin and created a diffused light that entered the room and created a soft glow of peace. My favorite thing to watch was an iron wagon that was a music box that played "Home on the Range." It wound up from the back, and the wagon would move forward and backward as if coming out through a tunnel. You could hear the high tinging sound of the music box mechanism plucking away as well as the whirring white noise of the gears that made the wagon move along to the music. That wagon was the thing I was blessed to inherit when they died.

I also loved the backyard! It was big with a covered, detached porch area, and a small portion of a creek ran through the middle and was exciting to jump over. (It wasn't really that big.) There was also a mature tree from which hung a swing composed of a simple piece of wood tied with a thick rope that you had to straddle in order to swing. The rope went through the wood and had a great big knot underneath so that the rope would not break or come out from the wood piece, making it a sturdy, safe, homemade swing. There was also a fire pit where we would roast our traditional Easter hotdogs while all of us grandkids were running around finding all the flashes of colored eggs peeping up from the ground or slyly sitting on a window sill.

We would gather together for family parties to celebrate Easter and occasionally Christmas Eve. One Christmas, I remember my Gramps standing up out of his chair while he was singing a love song, and he went to hold my Grammy and continued to turn her around, gently and sweetly. It was a beautiful thing to watch. Gramps served in World War II, worked for Geneva Steel, and helped to put the "G" on the mountain in Pleasant Grove, Utah.

My Grammy loved the color purple! She loved playing games, especially Yahtzee, and putting puzzles together. She was a giver and loved everyone, making sure that everyone else was happy and taken care of before she would even consider thinking of herself. I am so grateful that I was able to have had about sixteen years of my life with great-grandparents.

Gathering Fast Offerings

By Leon Jensen

A Tribute to Leo Nelson, Early 1973

I was raised on a farm outside of a little town in Northern Utah called Bear River City. One of my responsibilities as a young Aaronic Priesthood holder was to go out and collect fast offerings. I remember that Leo Nelson was in my first assigned route. He was an elderly man who lived alone. I was surprised to see his name on my list. I hadn't seen him at church. In fact, I didn't remember ever seeing him at all up till that time. I didn't even think he was a member of our Church. However, I knew the stories about him, and the tales that young people had told made him seem mysterious and even scary.

I wish I could say that like Nephi of old, I knew that God had assigned me to do this and so I knew I could do it. However, the truth was, my faith just wasn't that strong. What I did have, though, was an implicit trust in my father. I remember voicing my concerns to my dad, and he encouraged me and told me to be brave, saying everything would work out to be okay. Thus, with trepidation I headed out to collect fast offerings.

It was less than a mile to Leo's place, but it seemed like a whole lot longer as I rode my bike, thinking about what could happen, knowing the stories I had heard. When I got there, I took a deep breath, said a little prayer, gathered what courage I could, then walked up to the door and knocked.

No answer.

I must admit, I was thinking that a good outcome would be that he wasn't home or just didn't answer the door. I was safe. *Perfect,* I thought. I had fulfilled my responsibility. However, that gentle little voice inside me said, "Knock again."

I reluctantly turned around, took another deep breath, and knocked again, this time a little louder. I waited, but again no answer. Just as I was about to turn around and leave, the door creaked open. *No turning back now,* I thought.

An elderly man invited me in. As I walked in, I could hardly breath, the tobacco smoke was so thick. But remembering my father's promise, I collected my thoughts and stated my purpose for coming. He asked me who

I was, and I could see the recognition in his face when I told him who my father was. He asked me to wait and headed into the other room.

After a little while, he appeared again with a wallet in his hand, from which he pulled out a couple of dollars and gave them to me. I was a little surprised at his willingness to donate. However, by this time the fear had left me, and I stood there wondering who this man really was whom the rumors had treated so unkindly. It was obvious by his surroundings that he didn't have a lot, but he gave out of what little he had. He asked me a couple of questions which I answered, and then I was on my way. As I walked outside, I took a deep breath of the fresh air. I struggled with asthma in my youth and wondered how the smoke would affect me, but my dad had said I would be okay, and I was.

Gathering fast offerings at Leo's place became a part of my permanent assignment. He would always give, even though it was clear he didn't have much to spare. Each time I would go, we would talk a little bit. He would ask me about my life, and it was obvious that he had a genuine interest. He really cared, and each month I went, I would leave having learned something. I always felt good when I would go there, and I never left feeling like I should not have come. I didn't know how it was possible, but my lungs never seemed to suffer because of my visits, even though the smoke was always thick. The only thing I can say is that my father's promise worked.

While it may not be hard to understand where the stories and rumors came from, I found them to be just that—simply rumors and not based in fact. Over the next months and years, I learned to love this man who from outward appearances did not seem to be living the commandments.

I did not realize it at first, but later as I thought about it, I realized that I always felt the Spirit when I visited Leo. I wondered how that could be, but the answer was clear and resounding: we all have sins and fall short. We do not have the right, nor the capability, to judge others. Only God knows what is truly going on and what is in our heart.

Leo was one of the kindest people I know. I have often found myself on my knees praying for his behalf. I am a better person, a more faithful person, a more righteous person, than I would have been had I not known Leo. I may not be able to say that Leo was perfect, but that is not for me to say anyway. He had an effect for good on my life. After all, isn't that what we're supposed to do if we are living our religion?

Thank you, Leo. Thank you.

Two Angels

By Rosalee Thain
For Mom and Dad's 60th wedding anniversary

Two angels sat in heaven above.
They spoke of life, they spoke of love.

We're going down to earth to dwell.
Will we meet there? I cannot tell.
How will you find me down below?
You must find me, I love you so.

Fear not, my love, for all is well.
The time and place I cannot tell.
But I'll find you, though for now we part,
For I hold you here, deep in my heart.

And so they left, on earth to roam,
Each sent to live in a loving home.
With brothers, sisters, parents too,
They grew up loving, faithful, true.

Their lives were good, though incomplete,
Until one day, they chance to meet.
A spark ignited in each heart.
They knew this was a brand new start.

Soon they wed in the house of God,
Built strong their life, held to the rod.
They welcomed a daughter, then a son.
Four others followed, one by one.

They raised these children, taught them well,
Then sent them off, their own tales to tell.
They watched them struggle with each choice.
As families grew, they did rejoice.

And now they sit back in their chair,
Content with what they've come to share.
As they look back, they're satisfied
They did their best at all they tried.

Now angels watch them from above,
Who had welcomed them to earth with love
And wait to welcome them back home,
For on that day, they'll no more roam.

And when they're gone and our thoughts turn
To memories sweet, our hearts will burn,
With hope and joy and love for them,
And we will know that once again . . .

Two angels sit in heaven above.
They speak of life, they speak of love.

One Enchanted Evening

By Janet Winward
February 1978

Even though there was snow on the ground, the sky was clear and inviting. The air was deceptively cold outside, but inside the Bear River City Recreation Hall, it was warm and comforting, all decked out in pleasant peaceful greens and bright glowing golds. The band was live, the hall was grand, the music was sweet and lively.

I was dressed more elegantly than I had been in many years, in a beautiful silky blue-green dress, with my hair all done up on top of my head and a decorative pin in the back. I felt young, like a princess in a fairy tale. The only thing that could improve on this kind of evening for someone like me, who loved to dance, would be the perfect partner. And there he was, my date for the evening.

He was young and handsome, charming and polite, tall and strong, a gentlemen all the way. His deep blue eyes were set off by the pale blue shirt under his dark suit. And did he ever know how to dance! He knew the steps, the moves, and how to lead a lady across the floor. I was sure grateful that my father had taught me how to follow a good dancer. The press of his hand on my waist was warm, firm, but gentle as he led me from one dance to another. I glided in my stocking feet across the highly polished wood floor. I didn't know all the steps, but no one would have known. He really knew how to make a girl look good out there dancing.

It was a fairy-tale evening. I had stepped into a dream. It didn't even matter that he was fifteen years younger than me. Tonight I was young and beautiful. Tonight I felt graceful and elegant. The evening was enchanted.

Leon had needed a date for this last dance before he left on his mission. He didn't want any girls he had dated previously to get any wrong ideas. And the town . . . well, you know the gossip in a small town—the girl he takes to the last dance before he leaves! He wanted to be careful and leave nothing for their imaginations. His sister Mary Ellen had told him how I love to dance but rarely had the opportunity, so he asked me to accompany him for this evening of evenings.

As the evening progressed, I could hear the whispers. "Who is the girl with Leon?" Some even came up suggesting an introduction, but he skillfully and tactfully maneuvered around their questions. He was having so much fun keeping them all in suspense. That just added to the joy that seemed to bubble all over inside me. I wanted to laugh out loud. There were many there who should have known me. After all, I grew up in Bear River City. I had been gone for several years, but it surprised me that no one seemed to recognize me. Apparently I was in an unexpected place and time, and they did not make the connection.

It had been many years since I had been to any dance, let alone the annual Gold and Green Ball in Bear River City. It was always one of the best events of the year. Dancing in this little town was a monthly event when I lived there. It all started in the early 1880s when C. C. Johnsen started a small orchestra and played for dances. Now, some ninety years later, the tradition had slowed some but continued to be a grand tradition. It started with the children's dances.

As the whispers went on through much of the evening, I wondered how long we could get away with this. I was surprised it had lasted this long. Who would be the first to figure it out? Who would finally recognize that Leon's date for this special last dance was actually . . . his big sister? They would have known me as Evelyn. The memory still thrills me.

I Am (Chapter 1)

By Donna Hill
2021

I am a lump of coal under pressure, a wannabe multifaceted diamond, split in many ways, many souls rolled into one with many sides in need of polish.

I am a depression child, frugal to a fault, who enjoys transforming the useless into something valuable.

Sometimes I am a cheerful, happy, resilient, and optimistic lady who can adjust to whatever comes my way and find good in it.

When needed, I am an encouraging, understanding, helpful ally of those who suffer, a comforting friend who feels the pain of others in their losses.

I am a proud mother and an adoring grandmother, contributing to the overabundance which leads to the downfall of the latest "me-first generation."

On a good day, I am an enthusiastic, fun-loving, energetic, capable party girl.

Some days I am a tottering, dependent senior citizen, a collection of anguish, frustration, and pain.

Sometimes I am a sweet young thing, living in an octogenarian's body, longing for someone special to talk to, to listen to, who thinks I am special too.

I'm even the child of my overprotective children at times.

Mostly at bedtime, I am a tired, cold, discouraged, lonely old lady, wondering what's the use. Then I start remembering and kneel and count blessings. I reminisce, reliving lovely days, sweet memories, happy times.

Then I am overwhelmed with gratitude and love, remembering the one thing that never changes: *I am a beloved daughter of God* who knows my name is Donna. I recognize His "coincidences," His tender mercies, His miracles. I feel His love and long to see His face again one day—but not just now. I'm not finished yet. I have miles to go and room to grow.

I Am (Chapter 2)

Donna Hill
2021

I am not an athlete; I'd rather sew than join the fray out there.
Afraid of balls, coming fast, toward me through the air.
Neither do I sing and dance extraordinarily swell,
And leading the singing reminds me of ____ well,
my very worst nightmare.
But how I love and admire those who do and share.
Their grace and beauty touch me as they expertly perform
And leave me feeling gratitude, comforted, and warm.

Preparing for Winter

By Donna Hill
2021

I've tasted the bitter and the sweet, seen my share of joy and strife.
It's October now, and I'm hunkering down for the winter of my life,
Canning, drying, freezing, storing up necessities
Like faith and hope and charity and opportunities
To help and serve and comfort those I see in need.
Preparation is the key if I am to succeed
And emerge in the spring to eternal new life
Devoid of worldly woes, earth cares, and senseless strife.

Mom's Chocolate Chip Cookies

By Shaylee Ray

"Girls! It's time to make some cookies!" My head snapped up as I heard my mother's voice, and a grin spread across my face. I replied with as much enthusiasm and volume as I could muster, "I'm coming!" That's when the thundering sound of six feet running down the hallway echoed through the house. One by one, we came to a stop by the island bar that was in our kitchen. My two younger sisters and I were so excited to make cookies with Mom! This was always a fun activity that we looked forward to.

We gazed over all of the ingredients: the buttery-smooth shortening, the fluffy flour, the sparkling sugar, the patiently waiting egg next to the bottle of the delicious-smelling vanilla, the bright orange box of baking soda, and the Morton girl with her bright red umbrella on the side of the salt container who seemed to be looking at the chocolate chips with eager delight!

"Alright, what comes first?" Mom asked. Ariana, Allison, and I jumped up to reach for the shortening, egg, sugars, and vanilla. We grabbed the measuring cups and carefully leveled off the shortening, cracked the egg, poured in the fragrant vanilla, and watched mesmerized as the sugar (both white and brown) fell like a snowy blizzard into the big macaroni-and-cheese-colored mixing bowl. At least the white sugar was like snow—the brown sugar fell flat into the bowl, holding the shape of the measuring cup it came out of as if its life depended on it.

All of us girls watched as our mother expertly whipped together the ingredients as if it was a light, fluffy cloud. Then we added in the flour, baking soda, and salt. Mom was definitely in charge of mixing at this point as our young arms weren't quite strong enough to whip the ingredients into the dough mix that clung to the outside edges of the mixing bowl like a spinning ride at a carnival.

"Okay, girls, now it's the best part!" Mom said with an enormous grin, anticipating our excitement.

"Chocolate chips!" we all enthusiastically answered together. It was indeed the best part. We measured out the amount for the cookies, and then, as our tradition dictated for every time we made cookies, we parceled some out to each of us to enjoy a chocolaty treat!

Once the cookie dough was nice and mixed together, we each helped to roll the dough into balls, taking care to make sure that each one had plenty of chocolate chips hidden inside and around the ball. Mom picked up the full cookie sheet and put it lovingly into the preheated oven. We all went to play a game together while we waited the 8–10 minutes of bake time for the cookies to be done. As the time got closer and closer to being done, the aroma of fresh-baked cookies became stronger and stronger until you could practically taste the cookies just by the smell!

The oven timer chimed its happy tune, and we jumped up for joy! "Yay! The first batch is done!" we exclaimed with our arms in the air. After waiting not-so-patiently for the cookies to cool, we were finally able to enjoy a fresh, homemade chocolate chip cookie. I took a bite and enjoyed the soft breaking of the cookie as it fell onto my tongue and relished the sweet, dark, sticky, melted chocolate as it filled my mouth with pleasure.

"Mom," I said with a satisfied grin, "I love your cookies, and I love you!" We all came together into a big hug. Our tummies were full of cookies, and our hearts were filled with love.

Mom's Chocolate Chip Cookies

⅔ cup butter shortening
½ cup granulated sugar (white sugar)
½ cup brown sugar (packed)
1 egg
1 tsp. vanilla
1½ cups flour
½ tsp. baking soda
½ tsp. salt
1 package of chocolate chips

Preheat oven to 375 degrees. Mix shortening, sugars, egg, and vanilla thoroughly. Stir in the dry ingredients together. Add chocolate chips. Drop rounded dough balls onto a greased cookie sheet. Bake 8–10 minutes. Cool on a wire rack. ENJOY!

Tips for Preparing a Memorable Picnic

By Donna Teeples
March 8, 2019

Nine years old seems young from my perspective now, but I felt pretty grown up to be able to go on a trip to California with my paternal grandparents. My older sister Janet was eleven and we were inseparable, so to be together on this trip was an anticipated adventure.

My grandfather owned an old model two-door coupe, and even for a nine- and eleven-year-old, there wasn't much room in the back because of the back slope of the car. I suppose the trip to California was pleasant enough. I can't really remember much of the long drive.

We were headed for my grandmother's sister's home in the mountains near Pasadena. It must have been early morning or late afternoon when we began our trek into the mountains, as the sun was low on the horizon and obscured somewhat by trees. As we ascended up the mountainous switch-backs, the sun flickered through the trees, and as I was prone to car sickness, the twists, turns, and flickering sunlight through the trees was a recipe for discomfort. I began to feel that uneasy upheaval in my stomach and had to keep swallowing the gathering saliva in my mouth to keep my food down. I became more squeamish with each turn, but I didn't want to be the cause of detaining my grandparents or to have them worry about me. My only thought was to get where we were going in great haste!

I felt confined in the small back seat with seemingly no air. My sister felt compassion for me but could do nothing to ease my suffering. By the time we arrived, I was more than miserable. I had to have help climbing out of the back seat, and all I wanted to do was rest for a while to calm the churning.

Janet and I had never met our grandmother's sister before, but she and her husband were kind and good-natured. They lived a simple life in their small home nestled among the trees, their wants being supplied by a garden, a cow, and a few other animals. I had my first taste of cold, raw milk and thought it was very refreshing. They showed us great hospitality.

One day they suggested a picnic on the beach of a nearby lake, and Janet and I were really excited. We were told we were going to have fried rabbit, which was foreign to our menu at home. We followed the man into the yard like puppies and watched as he caught one of the rabbits and tied its back legs to the clothes line. He did the same with another rabbit. Being city girls, we were not prepared for what happened next! This gentle man took a flat board and smacked the rabbit's head as though he were batting a ball. We were stunned! The eyes of the rabbit turned immediately pink and seemed to me to spiral around like is shown in cartoons. The process was repeated on the second rabbit. I felt immediately queasy. The rabbits quickly died from the blow. That was traumatic enough, but then he cut off their heads and threw them to his dog, and we watched and listened with abhorrence as the dog crunched the eyeballs! That apparently was too much for us because I don't remember any of the other preparations of skinning and butchering the rabbits. Grandma's sister fried the rabbits and prepared other food for our picnic.

My sister and I had a wonderful time at the picnic playing in the water, but neither of us had an appetite for Kentucky-fried rabbit!

As I look back on that trip, the rabbits immediately take front stage, but there were other things like the beautiful mountain scenery and crisp cool air that gladdened my heart. The hospitality of our hosts made us feel immediately welcome.

I regret that I don't remember more about the interaction with my grandparents on this trip. They were both rather quiet. My grandfather had a wonderful dry wit. They were in their mid-sixties at the time so they perhaps seemed old to us, but we always felt their kindness and their love. I am grateful for this memorable experience shared with my sister and our grandparents.

My Wrestle with Jealousy

By Diana Despain

Somewhere around 1985, while living in Clinton, Missouri, I had a very humbling experience. We had been moving about every two years because of work and landlords needing their houses back, and we were finally in a home we were able to purchase. We had moved to Clinton in 1979 from Hyde, Pennsylvania, where my husband Dennis had been working for the Clearfield Cheese Company. Before that, we lived in Billerica, Massachusetts. Dennis was hired to work in Boston for the mother company of Clearfield Cheese after graduating from Utah State University.

One day my mom called and told me about my sister and her family and how they had purchased a hobby farm in Hurricane, Utah. After we had a good visit and I hung up the phone, I cried and cried. I thought, "I'm the one who has dreamed about having a hobby farm, not my sister!" And also, "It's just not fair that she gets to have horses and not me!" When we were growing up in Montana, it was me who was always riding the horses. She would ask me to saddle them up when her friend came over to ride. I loved being outside with the animals, and I would go horseback riding everywhere I could! I think I even would have slept on the horse if my mom had allowed it!

When Sunday rolled around, I was still moping around, feeling sorry for myself. Dennis was branch president at the time and had a 6:30 a.m. meeting. Since we only had one car, I got up and drove him to the church, which was about five miles away. After dropping him off, I turned on the radio to listen to the *Music & the Spoken Word* broadcast, which luckily aired at that time each Sunday. The message shared that day is one that has stayed with me all these years. It sure humbled me and helped me see an eternal perspective in this emotional journey.

In the message, the speaker talked about those dreams and plans we hope to fulfill in our lives and how disappointed we are when they don't become a reality. Then he said, which hit me so powerfully, "Don't worry. If you have been serving the Lord and helping those around you and doing good things wherever you are, you will receive blessings beyond measure." Well, then to top it all off, when the message was finished, the Tabernacle Choir sang, "You'll Never Walk Alone." Of course, I cried all the way home! I thought about all the branches in the church we had been part of and served in and helped to strengthen the members. As I counted the blessings that had come through serving the Lord, a light came on and took away the darkness that I had allowed to envelop me. All of a sudden, I felt completely different about my life. I then cheered for my sister that she could live my dream! Really, it was more for her husband anyway!

I certainly learned that jealousy and bitterness can drive peace and happiness away from a person's heart. I didn't like the dark cloud that seemed to follow me all week long. Heavenly Father knew what I needed that day to help me gain an eternal perspective on this matter! I was in the right place at the right time!

Prophets Represent Jesus Christ

By Janet Winward

The year 1988 was a hard year for me, but 1989 proved to be a reward for surviving. I have always known that the prophets—through the Bible and in the latter days—are truly representatives of the Savior Jesus Christ, but an experience brought it strongly to my heart. Sister H., our stake Relief Society president, had a strong impression she needed to take the sisters of the stake on a Church history tour. Before this, that was something that was frequently done but had been stopped, so she had to go clear to the top to get permission.

The trip began on an airplane, then we traveled for ten days on two buses to Church history sites, ending in Carthage and Nauvoo for two days. I had many spiritual experiences during this time. I want to tell you about the one that happened at the end of the trip.

Our group of ninety sisters was divided onto two planes. I was the last one to get on our plane. Imagine my surprise when I rounded the corner, walked through first-class to get to my seat, and saw on the front seats President Ezra Taft Benson and his wife! I reached and shook his hand, and he acted as if I were a long-lost friend. The other sisters all had the same experience.

The group on the other plane was greeted by President Gordon B. Hinckley, who was President Benson's First Counselor at that time.

Not too long before arriving in Salt Lake, we experienced some turbulence. The seat belt signs came on. My first thought was, "If it's time for the prophet to go, I'll be glad to go with him." I just relaxed.

When we arrived in the Salt Lake airport, our families were there waiting. (This was before all the crazy security, so those meeting us could come straight to the gate.) Most of the forty-five sisters on my flight had young children who would be meeting them. After nearly two weeks, they would surely be excited to see their mothers, right?

When the plane arrived, of course the first-class people disembarked first. President and Sister Benson were taken on an airport electric cart. When *we* left the plane, none of the children even noticed! They were all joyfully, reverently gathered around the prophet. Children who had come with excitement to see their returning mothers were now enfolded in the love of the Savior.

President Ezra Taft Benson was paying special attention to the children. The feeling in that section of the airport was so strongly spiritual. I don't believe anyone could have been so hardhearted to miss it. Those children knew who he was. He was a prophet of God and they loved him. I had the feeling I was in the presence of the Savior surrounded by the children. I wish I could explain the feeling, the strength of the Spirit. I was deeply moved. I know the Savior's emissary was there, and so did those children. They felt the Savior's love that day as I did, as it warmed me to my very core. Even now as I write this, the tears flow. The Spirit that day was so strong, it has stayed with me all these years.

Notes

1. Alex Haley, "In every conceivable manner," BrainyQuote, accessed Dec. 7, 2022, https://www.brainyquote.com/quotes/alex_haley_391545.
2. Russell M. Nelson, "Open the Heavens through Temple and Family History Work," *Ensign*, Oct. 2017.
3. Dale G. Renlund, "Consider the Goodness and Greatness of God," *Ensign* or *Liahona*, May 2020, 41–44.
4. Stephen Leacock, *Delphi Complete Works of Stephen Leacock (Illustrated)* (East Sussex: Dephi Classics, 2018).
5. AMA Staff, "The Lightning Bug vs. the Lightning," American Management Association, Jan. 24, 2019, https://www.amanet.org/articles/the-lightning-bug-vs-the-lightning/.
6. Mark Twain, *Following the Equator: A Journey Around the World* (Hartford, CT: American Publishing Company, 1898), 156.
7. "Self-improvement," Talk Teach Inspire, accessed Dec. 7, 2022, https://talk-teachinspire.com/self-improvement/.
8. Lucy Crichton, "Fiction Ed's Blog: Anthony Trollope's Writing Advice," The People's Friend, Apr. 19, 2022, https://www.thepeoplesfriend.co.uk/2022/04/19/fiction-eds-blog-anthony-trollope-writing-advice/.
9. Craig L. Foster, "The Butler Murder of 1869: A Look at The Extralegal Punishment in Utah," *Mormon Historical Studies* 2, no. 2 (Fall 2001): 105–114. https://ensignpeakfoundation.org/wp-content/uploads/2013/05/Mhs2.2FosterFall2001.pdf.
10. Hello.misssunshine, "You are allowed to fail," Facebook, May 25, 2022, https://www.facebook.com/watch/?v=323614093108599.
11. William James, "Act as if what you do," BrainyQuote, accessed Dec. 7, 2022, https://www.brainyquote.com/quotes/william_james_105643.
12. John L. Sorenson, "Mormon's Miraculous Book," *Ensign*, Feb. 2016.
13. "Remember: Your lifeguard walks on water," Brittany Mooney, Apr. 25, 2013, https://brittanymooney.wordpress.com/2013/04/25/remember-your-lifeguard-walks-on-water/.
14. Henry B. Eyring, "Gathering the Family of God," *Ensign* or *Liahona*, May 2017, 22.

15. This painting can be seen in the following article: Quentin L. Cook, "Church History: A Source of Strength and Inspiration," *Ensign*, July 2020.

16. Billy Graham, "Life without God," accessed Dec. 7, 2022, https://www.azquotes.com/quote/851442.

17. "The Second Great Commandment," Shanon Brooks, Feb. 2013, https://shanonbrooks.com/2013/02/the-second-great-commandment/.

18. Jeffrey R. Holland, "An Ensign to the Nations," *Ensign* or *Liahona*, May 2011, 113.

19. Andy Murphy, "One Mexican Fisherman — One American Businessman — 3 Profound Life Lessons," Medium, Mar. 9, 2022, https://medium.com/illumination/one-mexican-fisherman-one-american-businessman-3-life-lessons-ea978c0a2430.

20. Sue Fitzmaurice, "I'm not interested in whether," Quotefancy, accessed Dec. 7, 2022, https://quotefancy.com/quote/2634565/.

21. Thomas A. Edison, "I have not failed," BrainyQuote, accessed Dec. 7, 2022, https://www.brainyquote.com/quotes/thomas_a_edison_132683.

22. Vivan Greene, "Life isn't about waiting," Goodreads, accessed Dec. 7, 2022, https://www.goodreads.com/quotes/132836.

23. Richard G. Scott, "Finding Joy in Life," *Ensign*, May 1996, 24.

24. Mother Teresa, "It's not how much we give," Goodreads, accessed Dec. 7, 2022, https://www.goodreads.com/quotes/20324.

25. Lori Deschene, "35 Inspirational Facebook Cover Quotes," The Simplicity Habit, accessed Dec. 7, 2022, https://www.thesimplicityhabit.com/facebook-cover-quotes/.

26. Alex Haley, "Every death," Quotefancy, accessed Dec. 7, 2022, https://quotefancy.com/quote/1221413/.

27. Sarah Jane Weaver, "Episode 69: Elder Christofferson and President and Sister Top emphasize drawing courage from history to face modern challenges," *Church News*, Feb. 8, 2022, https://www.thechurchnews.com/2022/2/8/23218898/elder-d-todd-christofferson-president-brent-l-top-sister-wendy-c-top-mormon-battalion-episode-69.

28. Xone Media, Twitter post, Nov. 19, 2016, 7:02 AM, https://twitter.com/Xone_Media/status/799976134322556929.

29. Jeffrey R. Holland, "For Times of Trouble" (Brigham Young University devotional, Mar. 18, 1980), 10, speeches.byu.edu.

30. Amanda Rose, "A Meaningful Life Is Not About Being Rich," Mind Journal, accessed Dec. 7, 2022, https://themindsjournal.com/a-meaningful-life-is-not-about-being-rich/.

31. Russell M. Nelson, "Sisters' Participation in the Gathering of Israel," *Ensign* or *Liahona*, Nov. 2018, 69.

32. Spencer Williams, "Faith Helped Pioneers Thrive, Elder Corbridge Says at Days of '47 Sunrise Service," *Church News*, July 25, 2019.

33. Carol White, "Keep Your Head Up Quotes to Get You Through Hard Times," accessed Dec. 7, 2022, https://bestwishesandquotes.com/keep-your-head-up-quotes/.

34. Ernest Hemingway, "We are all apprentices," BrainyQuote, accessed Dec. 7, 2022, https://www.brainyquote.com/quotes/ernest_hemingway_396672.

35. Dieter F. Uchtdorf, "The Infinite Power of Hope," *Ensign* or *Liahona*, Nov. 2008, 22.

36. "Importance of Record Keeping," *The Utah Genealogical and Historical Magazine, Volumes 7-9* (Salt Lake City: Genealogial Society of Utah, 1916), 98.

37. Henry B. Eyring, "Raise the Bar" (Brigham Young University–Idaho devotional, Jan. 25, 2005), byui.edu.

38. "President Hinckley Dedicates Mountain Meadows Monument," *Ensign*, Nov. 1999.

39. Maya Angelou, "You can't use up creativity," Goodreads, accessed Dec. 7, 2022, https://www.goodreads.com/quotes/153929.

40. *Saints: The Story of the Church of Jesus Christ in the Latter Days*, vol. 1, *The Standard of Truth, 1815–1846* (2018), xvii.

41. John Holmes, "There is no exercise better," Goodreads, accessed Dec. 7, 2022, https://www.goodreads.com/quotes/28364.

42. southwarkyas, "Your best is enough," Instagram, Sept. 18, 2021, https://www.instagram.com/p/CT9g4NYI4bM/.

43. Sukhraj Dhillon, "Always believe," Goodreads, accessed Dec. 7, 2022, https://www.goodreads.com/quotes/719934.

44. Rachel J. Trotter, "Writing a personal history, journal ideas and why it's important," LDS 365, Aug. 12, 2019, https://lds365.com/2019/08/12/writing-a-personal-history-journal-ideas-and-why-its-important/.

45. Ralph Waldo Emerson, "All life is an experiment," Goodreads, accessed Dec. 7, 2022, https://www.goodreads.com/quotes/251473.

46. Mandy Hale, Twitter post, Nov. 25, 2014, 4:27 PM, https://twitter.com/thesinglewoman/status/537387023968260096.

47. See Henry B. Eyring, "O Remember, Remember," *Ensign* or *Liahona*, Nov. 2007, 66–69.

48. Adapted from a popular quote by an unknown author.

49. Alex Haley, "In all of us there is a hunger," Goodreads, accessed Dec. 7, 2022, https://www.goodreads.com/quotes/25682.

50. Bruce Feiler, "The Stories That Bind Us," *The New York Times*, Mar. 15, 2013, https://www.nytimes.com/2013/03/17/fashion/the-family-stories-that-bind-us-this-life.html.

51. "How Great Thou Art," *Hymns*, no. 86.

About the Author

Janet E. Winward has put her heart and soul into encouraging others to record the stories that make up their lives. Classes she has been teaching since 2008 are partially combined in this book, making her amazing talent available to anyone with a spark of desire.

Open the pages and let your spark ignite into a fire of passion as she teaches you how to find the stories in your life, share who you really are, and do so in a way that will bring light to your life and leave a legacy of fun-to-read stories.

Scan to visit

www.storiestheywilllove.com